James Joyce: A Very Short Introduction

VERY SHORT INTRODUCTIONS are for anyone wanting a stimulating and accessible way into a new subject. They are written by experts, and have been translated into more than 45 different languages.

The series began in 1995, and now covers a wide variety of topics in every discipline. The VSI library currently contains over 650 volumes—a Very Short Introduction to everything from Psychology and Philosophy of Science to American History and Relativity—and continues to grow in every subject area.

Very Short Introductions available now:

ABOLITIONISM Richard S. Newman
THE ABRAHAMIC RELIGIONS
    Charles L. Cohen
ACCOUNTING Christopher Nobes
ADOLESCENCE Peter K. Smith
ADVERTISING Winston Fletcher
AERIAL WARFARE Frank Ledwidge
AESTHETICS Bence Nanay
AFRICAN AMERICAN
    RELIGION Eddie S. Glaude Jr
AFRICAN HISTORY John Parker and
    Richard Rathbone
AFRICAN POLITICS Ian Taylor
AFRICAN RELIGIONS
    Jacob K. Olupona
AGEING Nancy A. Pachana
AGNOSTICISM Robin Le Poidevin
AGRICULTURE Paul Brassley and
    Richard Soffe
ALEXANDER THE GREAT
    Hugh Bowden
ALGEBRA Peter M. Higgins
AMERICAN BUSINESS HISTORY
    Walter A. Friedman
AMERICAN CULTURAL
    HISTORY Eric Avila
AMERICAN FOREIGN
    RELATIONS Andrew Preston
AMERICAN HISTORY Paul S. Boyer
AMERICAN IMMIGRATION
    David A. Gerber
AMERICAN INTELLECTUAL HISTORY
    Jennifer Ratner-Rosenhagen

AMERICAN LEGAL HISTORY
    G. Edward White
AMERICAN MILITARY
    HISTORY Joseph T. Glatthaar
AMERICAN NAVAL HISTORY
    Craig L. Symonds
AMERICAN POLITICAL
    HISTORY Donald Critchlow
AMERICAN POLITICAL PARTIES
    AND ELECTIONS L. Sandy Maisel
AMERICAN POLITICS
    Richard M. Valelly
THE AMERICAN PRESIDENCY
    Charles O. Jones
THE AMERICAN REVOLUTION
    Robert J. Allison
AMERICAN SLAVERY
    Heather Andrea Williams
THE AMERICAN SOUTH
    Charles Reagan Wilson
THE AMERICAN WEST Stephen Aron
AMERICAN WOMEN'S HISTORY
    Susan Ware
AMPHIBIANS T. S. Kemp
ANAESTHESIA Aidan O'Donnell
ANALYTIC PHILOSOPHY
    Michael Beaney
ANARCHISM Colin Ward
ANCIENT ASSYRIA Karen Radner
ANCIENT EGYPT Ian Shaw
ANCIENT EGYPTIAN ART AND
    ARCHITECTURE Christina Riggs
ANCIENT GREECE Paul Cartledge

Available soon:

For more information visit our website

www.oup.com/vsi/

Colin MacCabe

JAMES JOYCE

A Very Short Introduction

OXFORD
UNIVERSITY PRESS

OXFORD
UNIVERSITY PRESS

Great Clarendon Street, Oxford, OX2 6DP,
United Kingdom

Oxford University Press is a department of the University of Oxford.
It furthers the University's objective of excellence in research, scholarship,
and education by publishing worldwide. Oxford is a registered trade mark of
Oxford University Press in the UK and in certain other countries

First edition published in 2021

Impression: 1

Published in the United States of America by Oxford University Press
198 Madison Avenue, New York, NY 10016, United States of America

British Library Cataloguing in Publication Data
Data available

Library of Congress Control Number: 2021938256

ISBN 978-0-19-289447-2

Printed in Great Britain by
Ashford Colour Press Ltd, Gosport, Hampshire

For Bobby Bress. Great student,
great driver, great friend.
And
For Finn and Beatrice, Triestini

Contents

List of illustrations

Abbreviations

Works by Joyce

Crit.	James Joyce. *Occasional, Critical and Political Writing*. Edited by Kevin Barry. Oxford: Oxford University Press, 2000.
D	James Joyce. *Dubliners*. Edited by Jeri Johnson. Oxford: Oxford University Press, 2000.
FW	James Joyce. *Finnegans Wake*. Edited by Robbert-Jan Henkes, Erik Bindervoet, and Finn Fordham. Oxford: Oxford University Press, 2012.
Letters I–III	James Joyce. *Letters of James Joyce*. Edited by Stuart Gilbert [vol. 1] and Richard Ellmann [vols 2 & 3]. London: Faber and Faber, 1957–66.
P	James Joyce. *A Portrait of the Artist as a Young Man*. Edited by Seamus Deane. London: Penguin, 1992.
SH	James Joyce. *Stephen Hero*. Edited by Theodore Spencer, John J. Slocum, and Herbert Cahoon. New York: New Directions, 1955.
U	James Joyce. *Ulysses*. Edited by Declan Kiberd. London: Penguin, 1992.

Other Works

Conv.   Arthur Power. *Conversations with James Joyce*.
              Edited by Clive Hart. New York: Barnes and
              Noble, 1974.

HJW   *How Joyce Wrote* Finnegans Wake: *A
              Chapter-by-Chapter Guide*. Edited by Luca
              Crispi and Sam Slote. Madison: University of
              Wisconsin Press, 2007.

JJ   Richard Ellmann. *James Joyce*. 2nd edn. London:
              Faber and Faber, 1982.

JWK   *The Joyce We Knew*. Edited by Ulick O'Connor.
              2nd edn. Dingle: Brandon, 2004.

MBK   Stanislaus Joyce. *My Brother's Keeper*. London:
              Faber and Faber, 1958.

Mim.   Erich Auerbach. *Mimesis: The Representation of
              Reality in Western Literature*. Princeton:
              Princeton University Press, 1953.

UA   Don Gifford with Robert J. Seidman. Ulysses
              Annotated: Notes for James Joyce's Ulysses. 2nd
              edn. Berkeley: University of California Press, 2008.

James Joyce

1. This statue of Joyce crossing the Canal Grande in Trieste was commissioned to mark the centenary of Joyce's arrival in the city.

Chapter 1
A publication in post-First World War Paris

In the evening of 1 February 1922, the printer Maurice Darantière approached the railway station in Dijon with a packet containing two copies of the book that he had finished printing the day before. He had originally suggested that he would put the copies straight in the express post which would be in Paris the next day. However, the author was extraordinarily superstitious and had become convinced that the book's success was dependent on it being published on his birthday, Candlemas Day. He urged the publisher to find a more secure method. The resourceful printer came up with another stratagem. He would entrust the books to the conductor of the newly inaugurated Train Bleu night train which would reach Paris in the morning where they could be picked up by the publisher. The train reached Paris at 7 a.m. and Sylvia Beach, the young American bookseller who was publishing her first book, was there to meet it. She rushed to the author's flat and presented him with his fortieth birthday present. Then she rushed to her bookshop, Shakespeare and Company, and displayed the second copy in the window. The book was *Ulysses*, the author James Joyce, and its publication was, for the English language, the major literary event of the 20th century.

In 1922 James Joyce occupied an unprecedented position in world letters. He was so famous that even Winston Churchill had subscribed for the de luxe limited first edition of *Ulysses*. Perhaps more pertinently both Ezra Pound and T. S. Eliot held him to be the greatest master of prose fiction writing in English. He had already attracted generous support both public (the British state had granted him a pension, at the urging of W. B. Yeats) and private (a Rockefeller daughter had gifted him considerable sums). Even more significant a leftist feminist called Harriet Shaw Weaver had decided that she would devote most of her considerable fortune to supporting the man she considered to be the most important contemporary English writer, perhaps the crucial figure in the revolution that was at hand. However, this world famous figure had few readers. The most important reason for this was the very widespread desire to destroy his writings before they could be read. Several chapters of *Ulysses* had been destroyed by officials charged with extirpating anarchist subversion in the United States. More personally the longest and most difficult chapter of *Ulysses*, Circe, had been thrown into a fire by an irate husband who started reading what his wife was engaged in typing up as fair copy. But perhaps the incident which best captures the fear and loathing that Joyce's writing produced occurred in 1912 when a Dublin printer was so offended by Joyce's portrait of their native city that he preferred to pulp the volumes of *Dubliners* he had printed rather than allow their author to buy them from him.

This marked the low point of Joyce's literary fortunes. He had completed the collection of twelve short stories in 1905, at the young age of 23, and they had been accepted for publication. However, when he added two new stories, one of them, 'Two Gallants', so offended both publisher and printer (and under English law both publisher and printer were liable for publishing obscene material) that they refused to set it in type. When Joyce rather unwisely pointed out that many of the other stories were much worse, he set in train a correspondence both farcical and horrific in which more and more cuts were demanded of him and this ended, after four years, with the English publisher reneging on his agreement. It was a subsequent agreement with a new Irish publisher which came to an end with the outraged printer preferring to forgo any income for his endeavours in favour of the pleasure of informing the author that he was going to pulp all the copies of his immoral and unpatriotic book. When faced with this heartbreaking conclusion to seven years of trying to get his short stories published, Joyce left Dublin for good.

The theme of exile is central to much of Joyce's work. It provides one of the emphases of the closing pages of *A Portrait of the Artist as a Young Man*: 'I will tell you what I will do and what I will not do. I will not serve that in which I no longer believe, whether it calls itself my home, my fatherland, or my Church: and I will try to express myself in some mode of life or art as freely as I can and as wholly as I can, using for my defence the only arms I allow myself to use—silence, exile, and cunning' (268). These words which are set in 1902 were not written until more than ten years later when Joyce had indeed decided to leave his country for good. But his original exile in Paris (the culmination of the final section of *A Portrait*) ended after a few months with a telegram: *Mother dying Come home father*. (In the 1984 Gabler edition of *Ulysses* this line is printed as 'Nother dying come home father'. To adopt this reading is to accept that Joyce's obsessive checking of proofs did not extend to one of the most important lines in the text. Fuller references to the Gabler edition can be found in Further Reading.)

This first return to Ireland provided the subject matter for *Ulysses* set in 16 June 1904, the day on which his life was joined to Nora Barnacle, who would be his life companion and with whom he would leave Dublin in the autumn of that year. Many commentators take the fictional Stephen Dedalus at his word and see Joyce determined on the spiritual condition of exile from very early on. However, when he left Dublin in 1904 his exile was propelled by much more temporal considerations and was by no means as definitive as it became in retrospect. Exile has been the condition of the majority of Irish men and women for over two centuries as they have fled poverty and hunger to find work across the globe. Joyce was merely joining his countrymen when, unable to earn a living in Dublin, he set out to find work as a language teacher in Europe.

He was much more individual, however, in that this economic imperative was intensified by questions of sexuality. Joyce's rejection of the Catholic Church in which he had been reared was so visceral that on his return from Paris he refused his dying mother's entreaties to kneel and pray at her deathbed. When he determined to spend his life with the young woman from Galway who had made out with such enthusiasm on 16 June, he had no intention of marrying her with the blessing of either Church or state. As he wrote later to his brother Stanislaus, 'I cannot tell you how strange I feel sometimes in my attempt to live a more civilized life than my contemporaries. But why should I have brought Nora to a priest or lawyer to make her swear away her life to me?' (*Letters II*, 89). But there was no question of Joyce living in Dublin with a woman to whom he was not married. It posed intermittent difficulties on the Continent; it would have been impossible in Catholic Ireland.

However, Joyce did think of moving back to Ireland in his early years in Trieste, where he worked at the Berlitz school, and his permanent exile was a state which was reached gradually. The overwhelming hostility which greeted his desperate attempts to publish *Dubliners* in Ireland in 1912 marked the final break with his homeland, but perhaps the most important symbolic moment had come on a visit he made three years earlier. He had come back to Dublin in the summer of 1909 both to secure an Irish publisher for *Dubliners* and also to see if there was any possibility of a professorship at his old university, but the visit was overwhelmed by a meeting with his old friend Cosgrave, who appears under the name of Lynch in both *A Portrait* and *Ulysses*. Cosgrave told Joyce that in the summer of 1904 as Joyce was pledging his life to Nora, Nora was also granting Cosgrave sexual favours. Joyce suffered a complete nervous collapse which is recorded vividly by his friend Byrne (Cranly in *A Portrait*). Byrne took Joyce to the house that he was living in at 7 Eccles Street and spent a whole afternoon convincing Joyce that Cosgrave's account was the product of spite and bitterness at the success that Joyce had made of his life with Nora and contained not one shred of truth. It is a testament to the importance of this moment in Joyce's psychic life that 7 Eccles Street appears in *Ulysses* as the house in which Leopold and Molly Bloom live and it is to that house that Leopold escorts Stephen Dedalus at the end of their long Dublin day.

Joyce never forgot the shock of believing himself cuckolded and spent the rest of his life trying to write his way out of that masculine desire for possession of the female body which he analyses in *Ulysses* as a part of the new forms of property inaugurated by capitalism. Crucial to this rewriting was the explosion of epistolary phone sex between Joyce and Nora occasioned by Joyce's initial belief in Cosgrave's claims. To read these letters between Trieste and Dublin in the summer of 1909 is to engage with a raw sexuality which Joyce will use as basic material for much of both the Circe and Penelope chapters of *Ulysses*. It is also to recognize a third reason why Joyce had to leave Dublin in 1904. He may have been disinclined to marry Nora Barnacle for ideological reasons but he would have found it more than difficult to marry her for social reasons in a Dublin still governed by Victorian morality. It is often remarked that it is difficult to marry across boundaries of race or nation, it is less often emphasized that to marry across class barriers is even more difficult.

Joyce's parents belonged to the Irish Catholic middle class, who had gained civil emancipation in 1829 but who were to be caught up in the struggle for political independence throughout the rest of the century. The struggle for Home Rule was to dominate Joyce's youth but the First World War saw violent revolution take the stage in 1916 and, after revolution and civil war, the establishment of the Irish Free State. His father John Stanislaus Joyce, an active participant in the Parnellite stage of this struggle in the 1880s, was a drunk and a wastrel who frittered away a substantial inheritance, and the family had lived in ever increasing poverty since Joyce was 10, a shift marked in *A Portrait* by the move from the middle-class suburbs of south Dublin to the slums north of the Liffey and in life by Joyce's move from an expensive boarding school, Clongowes, to a subsidized day school place at Belvedere.

But if the family moved irreversibly down the objective social ladder, John Stanislaus Joyce clung ever more fiercely to his imaginary social status. No son of his would marry a chambermaid at Finn's hotel who had been brought up by her grandmother in Galway. It was for this reason Joyce hid from his father that he was eloping with Nora when they took ship in the autumn of 1904 and indeed it was five years more before John Stanislaus Joyce was reconciled to his son's choice of lifelong companion. If Nora failed to measure up to notions of Victorian middle-class womanhood, she had been spared that extreme repression of the female body which was the Victorians' most astonishing contribution to civilization. One cannot imagine the well-brought-up young Sheehy girls who were from Joyce's own class, and one of whom provided the model for Miss Ivors in the final story of Dubliners 'The Dead', reacting very positively to a letter which evoked 'rank red cunt'; Nora, however, replied in kind.

After 1909 Joyce talked no more of returning permanently to Ireland but it was the horrendous visit of 1912 which rendered exile irreversible. It is difficult to read the account of Joyce's final desperate efforts at that time to get his book of short stories published without suffering on the young author's behalf. When the publisher Roberts, who had played with Joyce like a cat with a mouse, delivered the final legal opinion that the whole book was libellous, Joyce wrote to Nora, 'I read it and walked down the street feeling the whole future of my life slipping out of my grasp' (*Letters II*, 311). It was not just his publisher who had turned against him; his old friend Thomas Kettle, now a Member of Parliament, said that he 'thought the book would do harm to Ireland', and in a final twist of the knife his own solicitor turned against him (*JJ*, 329). At 23, when he had submitted the original manuscript, he had been one of the most promising young authors in Ireland; at 30 he looked as though he was finished. He was certainly finished with Ireland.

The next year his luck finally changed. Grant Richards, who had been the original English publisher, asked to reconsider the book and *Dubliners* was finally published to respectful reviews and no scandal in June 1914. The publication of *Dubliners* allowed Joyce to take up again *A Portrait of the Artist as a Young Man*, an autobiographical account of his young life in Dublin on which he had been working since 1904 but which the endless difficulties with *Dubliners* had left stalled at the third chapter. The impetus to finish the book and finish quickly came from Ezra Pound. Pound, an American who had been in London since 1908, had made himself the entrepreneurial and ideological chief of a one-man revolution to modernize both his and others' writing in order to transform the world. England was at the height of its political and economic power and also at the end of its empire. Ireland was the most destabilizing force in British life and Pound's first major intervention was to teach the former member of the Irish Republican Brotherhood W. B. Yeats to abandon the diction and manner of his Gaelic Twilight poetry and to write in modern English. It was this modernized Yeats who was to become the poet of the Irish Revolution, the author of 'Easter 1916' and 'Meditations in Time of Civil War'. It was Yeats who alerted Pound to Joyce.

If you were looking for fault lines in the collapse of the Victorian empire, Ireland was one, women were another. Pound was both a womanizer and a sexist but before either of those he was a critic desperate for outlets for the new writing that he was discovering. One editor who shared his literary aims was Dora Marsden who had been a major player in the terrorist stage of the suffragette struggle. She had finally found the suffragettes too limited in their revolutionary aims and had set up a magazine called *The Freewoman*, which placed its revolutionary hopes in a new writing that was going to blast the old false writing; which would stop war and allow same-sex love. The writing that would usher in the revolution. When *The Freewoman* started its long fight with English printers to publish *A Portrait of the Artist* it had changed its name to *The Egoist*, after a brief spell as *The New Freewoman*, and was effectively edited by Harriet Shaw Weaver, who was to transform Joyce's life. Unlike almost all the other women who dedicated their lives to publishing Joyce, Harriet Shaw Weaver was not a flamboyant lesbian. She was often taken by the ordinariness of her dress to be a Quaker, but she had been reared in a Church of England vicarage. She had become both a feminist and a leftist (indeed she would finally join the Communist Party in 1938, the year before Joyce published *Finnegans Wake*).

History relates only one love in Harriet Shaw Weaver's life: as she published *A Portrait* chapter by chapter, she fell ecstatically in love with Joyce's writing. This was the greatest of writing, this was the new world glimpsed. Harriet Shaw Weaver was also on her mother's side a very considerable heiress and she determined that her contribution to the revolution would be to use her inheritance to allow Joyce to write as he pleased. In the end *A Portrait* could not be printed in London as a book but she imported copies from the United States. However, *A Portrait* was decorous compared to *Ulysses*. Grown men dropped their printing tools when they read 'snotgreen' and 'scrotumtightening' as new adjectives for the sea in the first chapter. By the time Joyce reached chapter 15, where the book's narrative climaxes in a brothel, our hero would change gender and the printers would have to be revived with smelling salts. More titillating, if less radical, the last chapter, no. 18, would be the semi-erotic reveries of a woman dozing next to her husband—he having visited a brothel that evening and she having committed adultery that afternoon. There could be no question of publishing *Ulysses* in England. No printer would touch it.

America, however, was more promising. The weight of censorship did not fall on printers and, in any case, there were scores of anarchist printers who would set anything that would blow the rotten system sky high. The American equivalent of the *Egoist* was the *Little Review* which was edited by two lesbians who had formed many of their ideas in the melting pot of feminism and anarchism. One of them, Jane Heap, is claimed by some to have written the first public defence of same-sex relationships. Both Heap and her lover Margaret Anderson were not fazed by the threat of imprisonment—they were happy to be imprisoned for the cause and determined, at whatever cost, to see *Ulysses* published. It is certain that the US authorities would have prosecuted chapter 15 of the novel, which is set in a brothel, but they didn't have to wait. Each chapter was being published in serial form with a title—the episode in the *Odyssey* to which it corresponded. Chapter 13 had the title Nausicaa.

The Nausicaa episode in the *Odyssey* reveals to us a beautiful young princess who has gone down to the sea with her attendants to launder bedding. Homer paints an erotic picture of an overexcited young virgin princess playing with her attendants when she is overwhelmed by the sight of the naked Odysseus arising out of the sea. The episode is one of the Western paradigms of the phallic warrior, the very idea which had just destroyed Europe. Joyce's version is less heroic. The chapter culminates with a beautiful young girl, her head full of romance, flashing her knickers at our hero, who takes the golden opportunity to furtively masturbate.

The United States may have ignored the printers but it was because they had developed a much more draconian system of censorship which concentrated on the distribution of obscene material through the post. The very real threat of anarchism in the first two decades of the 20th century combined with long-standing committees for the suppression of vice meant that censorship in the United States was terrifying in its reach and power. Nausicaa didn't stand a chance. John Quinn, Joyce's lawyer, kept Heap and Anderson, rather to their chagrin, out of jail but Nausicaa was banned and with it any chance of *Ulysses* being published in uncensored form in either America or England. It was Dublin in 1912 all over again but now Joyce was in Paris and had a young bookseller who worshipped Joyce's writing. Sylvia Beach would add publishing to her bookshop's many activities and the book would be published in Paris, the world centre of dirty books.

Production is one thing, distribution is another. The incredible stories of how many people risked prison to get *Ulysses* into both Britain and America is witness to how a book marketed to aesthetes was distributed by political believers. *Ulysses* was launched as a revolutionary text and it was to retain some of this aura for many decades. Joyce himself made no political pronouncements of any kind after he fled Trieste at the beginning of the First World War but his social world in Paris was that of the fellow travelling left.

The last two decades in Paris are unbearably sad. He was acknowledged as one of the most important writers in the world and Harriet Shaw Weaver's generosity meant that he lived like a rich man, with endless expensive holidays and Nora dressed in furs. His new project, which had the working title 'Work in Progress', was finally published in book form as *Finnegans Wake* by T. S. Eliot at Faber and Faber in 1939. He was undoubtedly the most influential writer in English of the 20th century. Eliot acknowledged *Ulysses* as having provided the method and inspiration for his great poem *The Waste Land*, and although Virginia Woolf and William Faulkner were less frank about their debts both *Mrs Dalloway* in 1925 and *The Sound and the Fury* in

1929 are clearly written in direct imitation of the opening chapters of *Ulysses*.

But Joyce could not really enjoy his years of fame for they were also years of growing blindness. He was plagued with constant attacks of iritis. The first had come in Trieste in 1907 and the second in Zurich in 1917 but in Paris there are operations and consultations every year if not every month. He was to lose almost all sight in one eye and needed a magnifying glass to write.

But there was worse to come. He was not only to experience the fading of physical light. His daughter Lucia, whose very name meant light, was to dissolve into madness during the 1930s. Joyce consulted psychiatrist after psychiatrist determined to convince them that his daughter's developing psychosis was simply experiments in language similar to those he was conducting in his own writing. It was the Swiss psychoanalyst Jung who delivered the most tragic judgement on this argument when he told the great author that he was diving but his daughter was drowning.

Nothing, however, would stop Joyce writing. Through blindness and madness, through the political turmoil of the 1930s as Europe prepared the second part of its fatal civil war, Joyce continued his most experimental work. There was this time no difficulty in getting his writing published either in instalments or in its final book form. In fact, *Finnegans Wake* is even more polymorphously perverse than *Ulysses*. However, it is written in an experimental language and the most complicated of narrative structures so that it needs to be studied at length to reveal its unspeakable sexual truths. Joyce's last book remains one of the great literary enigmas. Is it an irredeemably private work, a record of Joyce's own access to language and consciousness in the Dublin of the 1880s? Or is it, as he intended, a guide to the transformations and substitutions that constitute all of our dreaming minds? The jury is still out.

Finnegans Wake was published just before the outbreak of the Second World War and soon, for the second time in their lives, Joyce and Nora had to flee war and find refuge in neutral Zurich, the city where they had consummated their love in 1904. But now they were not the young lovers of that year nor the energetic family which had fled Trieste in 1915. Joyce was old beyond his years and his gargantuan abuse of alcohol was to take its final toll when a stomach ulcer perforated and he died on 13 January 1941.

There is no doubt that he is the greatest of all Irish writers. It is my opinion that he is the greatest of writers in English since Shakespeare. It is also the case that his writing deliberately attempts to undo the whole tradition of English literature stretching back to *Beowulf*. Joyce, however, is not like other writers of the Gaelic revival seeking in the past a pure Irish language and pure Irish bodies. All of Joyce's writing is a celebration of impurity, of what *Finnegans Wake* calls 'miscegenations on miscegenations' (*FW*, 18). Joyce's writing was intended above all as a contribution to a future which would not be paralysed and butchered by masculinity. His contribution has still to be fully measured.

Chapter 2
Dubliners

The end of the 19th century saw a massive increase in newspaper publication as the increasingly literate populations of the industrialized countries provided a huge market for a wide range of popular papers. One result of this development was an ever-increasing demand for short stories to leaven the news reporting which provided the majority of the content for this new form of newspaper. So valuable were these short stories in an ever more competitive marketplace that they provided very significant earnings for writers as diverse as Kipling, Chekhov, and de Maupassant.

Joyce too earned his first fee for fiction from one of these new media, but the *Irish Homestead* was not a mass tabloid publication and the fee which Joyce joyfully pocketed was a mere one pound. The *Irish Homestead* had been founded in 1895 as the paper of the Irish cooperative society, which promoted improvements in Irish agriculture through various forms of cooperative organization. One of the leaders of this movement was George Russell (Æ in *Ulysses*) who combined this commitment to agriculture with a devotion to theosophy and a fierce loyalty to literature. Although he did not become editor of the *Irish Homestead* until 1905, he seems to have acted as an informal editor for fiction and it was in that role that he wrote to Joyce having read and been impressed by some of the opening chapters of *Stephen Hero*, the autobiographical novel that Joyce was now engaged in writing. He knew that Joyce was desperate for money (which would prove a lifelong condition) and suggested that he might write a short story for the *Irish Homestead* which would be 'simple, rural? Livemaking? Pathos?' He added that the story should not shock the *Homestead*'s readers and that the paper would pay him a pound. 'It is easily earned money if you can write fluently and don't mind playing to the common understanding and liking for once in a way. You can sign it any name you like as a pseudonym' (*JJ*, 163).

Joyce referred scathingly to the *Irish Homestead* in *Ulysses* as the 'pig's paper' but he leapt at the opportunity that Russell so generously offered. Nor did his choice of pseudonym, Stephen Daedalus, suggest he was distancing himself from the story for this was the name that was already fully established as his fictional alter ego in the autobiographical novel which had impressed Russell. The story that he submitted was 'The Sisters'. It did not fit Russell's instructions to play to the common understanding and liking; still less was it simple or rural. But it was a paid-for publication and Joyce immediately announced that it was the first of a series of ten stories. 'I call the series Dubliners to betray the soul of that hemiplegia or paralysis that many consider a city' (*Letters I*, 55).

If the *Irish Homestead* crystallized the idea of a collection of stories which would take the city of Dublin as its subject, Joyce had long been writing preparatory sketches for such a project. His brother Stanislaus tells us that his first effort at writing as a schoolboy was called *Silhouettes* and that 'like the first three stories of *Dubliners* was written in the first person singular, and described a row of mean little houses along which the narrator passes after nightfall. His attention is attracted by two figures in violent agitation on a lowered window-blind illuminated from within, the burly figure of a man, staggering and threatening with upraised fist, and the smaller sharp faced figure of a nagging woman. A blow is struck and the light goes out. The narrator waits to see if anything happens afterwards. Yes, the window blind is illuminated again dimly, by a candle no doubt, and the woman's sharp profile appears accompanied by two small heads, just above the window, of children wakened by the noise. The woman's finger is pointed in warning. She is saying "Don't waken Pa'" (*MBK*, 104).

It is easy to imagine *Silhouettes* as a missing story from *Dubliners*; indeed it could be read as an alternative ending to 'Counterparts' in which the clerk Farrington takes out the frustrations of a day in which he is humiliated both in his office and in the pub, by beating his small son. These early sketches also demonstrate Joyce's deep distrust of narrative.

> Almost from the beginning, my brother followed his natural bent, which was for the plotless sketch. He came to consider a well ordered plot in a novel or story as a meretricious literary interest…More than he objected to the succession of thrilling incidents carefully worked out so as to keep the interest alive, my brother objected to the literary psychology which he found everywhere in fiction. He said that literature provided men and women with false consciences, literary consciences. *Silhouettes* was the first faint indication of that coming revolt of his against the hypocrisy of art. (*MBK*, 106)

While one can understand Stanislaus choosing the term 'plotless sketch' to describe *Dubliners*, it is misleading insofar as the narrative enigmas of *Dubliners* are due more to an overabundance of plot than to its artless absence. What is certain is that the majority of the simple stories in *Dubliners* are not susceptible to a straightforward narrative summary and the most learned of critics understand the stories in the most contradictory fashion. A good example of this is the story 'Eveline', which was the second story that Joyce published in the *Irish Homestead* in September 1904. The story opens with a young 19-year-old girl, Eveline, contemplating her life as she prepares to elope with a sailor,

Frank, whom she has met earlier in the summer and who has promised her a house and marriage in Buenos Aires where he has fallen on his feet. The second and much the shorter movement of the story is set at the North Wall where she is meant to board the ship with her husband to be. However at the last moment she is paralysed with indecision and she lets Frank board alone: 'He rushed beyond the barrier and called to her to follow. He was shouted at to go on but he still called to her. She set her white face to him, passive, like a helpless animal. Her eyes gave him no sign of love or farewell or recognition' (*D*, 29). For decades the story was read as another example of the paralysis that is the defining feature of Dublin life and the constant theme of Joyce's short stories.

Then, however, the critic Hugh Kenner concentrated his attention on a passage where Eveline is recalling her meetings with Frank and he noticed the appearance of two commas: 'He had fallen on his feet in Buenos Ayres, he said' (27). The commas around 'he said' signalled that the phrase 'He had fallen on his feet in Buenos Ayres' was Frank's and was an example of the kind of clichéd adventure narrative with which Eveline would have been familiar and which a practised seducer like Frank would have deployed many times before.

Suddenly Eveline's paralysis on the dock becomes not the ruin of a life but a lucky escape from what a Catholic like Kenner would have regarded as a fate worse than death. Rarely has a reading of two commas generated such critical fury. Critics to this day line up for or against Kenner. However, time and again in *Dubliners* we are confronted with alternative readings which cannot be resolved and if we consider the autobiographical background to Eveline we may find that ambiguity is constitutive to Eveline as it is to so many of the stories of *Dubliners*. Joyce published the story in September 1904 and in October 1904 he eloped with Nora Barnacle, who did not hesitate to board the ship at the North Wall.

At one level the story makes clear the enormous effort of will that propelled Nora to leave Ireland, although Eveline is not Nora, who had already left home in Galway and the threat of physical violence to make a life for herself in Dublin. But just as there are similarities between Nora and Eveline, there is some parallel between Joyce and Frank. On 10 June 1904, when Nora gave a back answer to a young man's palaver on Nassau street, she thought from his yachting cap that he was a sailor. Joyce was the assumed sailor and he courted Nora all that summer, which makes him an obvious original for Frank. If, however, we read Frank as Joyce we should notice that Kenner's reading becomes uncannily accurate. Joyce had no home in Buenos Aires. He also had no intention of marrying Nora. While he might lard this intention with fine words about not taking Nora to a priest or a lawyer to swear away her life, he was also carefully avoiding the legal responsibilities of matrimony. But to try to resolve Frank/Joyce into vile seducer or honest chap is to read against the multiple truncated narratives which refuse to resolve the characters of *Dubliners* into fixed identities. That these truncated narratives often mimic existing fictional forms does not alter the fact that they are never articulated together into what one might identify as a conventional story.

This is particularly evident in 'The Sisters', where there are endless hints of both a perverse relationship between the dead priest and the young boy and further intimations of earlier episodes of mental illness in the priest. It is, however, impossible to resolve these traces into a definite story which would fix boy and priest into a comprehensible bond. Indeed, the story makes savage fun of Old Cotter, who vaguely and vainly attempts such a resolution. These multiple narratives which defy any resolution are one of the key strategies of *Dubliners*.

A particularly good example is 'Two Gallants', one of the two stories (the other was 'A Little Cloud') that Joyce added to the original twelve that he had sent Richards in 1905. When we first

17

encounter Lenehan, whose yachting cap makes him one of the many versions of Joyce that populate *Dubliners*, he is listening to a story that is being related by his companion Corley. Corley's story remains a mystery to us as readers but we do learn that Corley has some kind of sexual assignation from which Lenehan hopes to benefit. This narrative lure floats over Corley's attempts to kill the time until he meets up with Lenehan after his tryst. When he does both we as readers and Lenehan have spent a great deal of time pondering the likelihood of Corley's success or failure. As readers however we have no idea of Corley's goal. The story ends with a crescendo of hope and despair as Lenehan rushes after a now solitary Corley, desperate to know his fate, while as readers we are simply desperate to know what the story has been about.

'Two Gallants' ends however as enigmatically as it began. To Lenehan's entreaties to tell all, Corley finally halts before a street lamp and 'with a grave gesture he extended a hand towards the light and, smiling, opened it slowly to the gaze of his disciple. A small gold coin shone in the palm' (*D*, 45). That we have been engaged in the commerce of money and sex has been evident from the beginning but this ending does not reveal whether Corley has persuaded his poor companion to part with her hard earned savings; to steal from her employer; or to engage in prostitution. Nor are we any the wiser as to what Lenehan's interest in the transaction is, why Corley might be in his debt.

This refusal of narrative closure so typical of *Dubliners* leaves the identity of the three protagonists opaque. But if narrative and identity fade, geography and history surge into view. Joyce is famously the poet of Dublin's streets and the long hours of Lenehan's patrol of those streets, while Corley accomplishes his mission, are a kind of prequel of *Ulysses*. It is not only the streets of Dublin that Joyce celebrates but also its food. There is no meal so keenly savoured in *Ulysses* as Lenehan's plate of peppered peas and ginger beer in the *Refreshment Bar* of Rutland Square.

This conjunction of place and food is a constant of Joyce's writing and perhaps its most memorable example in *Dubliners* comes when Maria, the elderly laundress who contributes one of the few sympathetic characters to the text of *Dubliners*, shops for her treasured cakes before her Halloween visit in 'Clay'. Composition of place is Joyce's bedrock, from the Flynn house in Great Britain Street where *Dubliners* begins to the hill of Howth where both *Ulysses* and *Finnegans Wake* end. But place in *Dubliners* is tightly tied to time. Joyce characterized his stories as a 'chapter in the moral history of my country' (*Letters* II, 134). 'Two Gallants' introduces us to the world of turn-of-the-century petit bourgeois homosocial Dublin from which Leopold Bloom is both excluded and excludes himself. It is the world which will be graphically described in one of the diary entries at the end of *A Portrait*: 'In company with Lynch followed a sizable hospital nurse. Lynch's idea. Dislike it. Two lean hungry greyhounds walking after a heifer' (*P*, 170).

The truncation and multiplication of narrative is not a guaranteed method of revelation. Quite the weakest story in the whole collection is 'After the Race' in which Jimmy Doyle, a provincial Dubliner fallen amongst foreign thieves, loses a fortune in a game of cards. We never know, as readers, whether Jimmy's foreign friends have conspired to lure him to the American yacht and the disastrous night of cards after the car race or whether the disaster is merely a matter of chance. More ambiguously still we do not know whether Jimmy has lost a lot of money or the entirety of his father's considerable riches. These suitably ambiguous narratives yield a memorable opening paragraph as 'The cars came scudding in towards Dublin, running evenly like pellets in the groove of the Naas Road' but we never gain any insight into the historicity of either the young European racing drivers or the Doyle family (*D*, 30). 'After the Race' is the only fiction where Joyce ventures outside lower-middle-class Dublin and he obviously knows as little about the merchant princes of his native city as about the racing drivers of Europe.

The other story in the collection that he judged a failure, 'A Painful Case', is, unlike 'After the Race', a masterpiece but it is a masterpiece in the form of realist fiction that Joyce had otherwise abandoned. The narrative of Duffy and Mrs Sinico and their failed relationship is neither truncated nor multiple and if it reveals much of its protagonists' individual psychology it says little of Dublin's geography and still less of the moral history of the country. James Duffy, unable to act on his emotions, bears an uncanny resemblance to Henry James's hero John Marcher in the almost exactly contemporaneous 'The Beast in the Jungle'. It will take Joyce a further fifteen years before he will be able in the Nighttown sequence of *Ulysses* to investigate the polymorphous perversity which underpins James Duffy's solitude. For *Dubliners* it remains one of the few stories written in a unified narrative voice.

It is this voice that Joyce consciously abandons in the opening paragraph of 'The Sisters', which he entirely rewrote for its book publication. The rewritten paragraph emphasizes the multiplication of narrative voices, none of which enjoys a hierarchical dominance over the other voices in the text. The paragraph is so important for *Dubliners* and indeed for Joyce's method in general that it is worth quoting both it and the *Irish Homestead* original in full:

(1) Three nights in succession I had found myself in Great-Britain Street at that hour, as if by Providence. Three nights also I had raised my eyes to that lighted square of window and speculated. I seemed to understand that it would occur at night. But in spite of the Providence that had led my feet, and in spite of the reverent curiosity of my eyes, I had discovered nothing. Each night the square was lighted in the same way, faintly and evenly. It was not the light of candles so far as I could see. Therefore, it had not yet occurred. (Opening paragraph of *Irish Homestead*)

(2) There was no hope for him this time: it was the third stroke. Night after night I had passed the house (it was vacation time) and

James Joyce

studied the lighted square of window: and night after night I had found it lighted in the same way, faintly and evenly. If he was dead, I thought, I would see the reflection of candles on the darkened blind for I knew that two candles must be set at the head of a corpse. He had often said to me: *I am not long for this world,* and I had thought his words idle. Now I knew they were true. Every night as I gazed up at the window I said softly to myself the word *paralysis.* It had always sounded strangely in my ears, like the word *gnomon* in the Euclid and the word *simony* in the Catechism. But now it sounded to me like the name of some maleficent and sinful being. It filled me with fear, and yet I longed to be nearer to it and to look upon its deadly work. (Opening paragraph of published text; *D*, 3)

The single voice of the *Irish Homestead* version is replaced by a split narrator who is both source and addressee ('I said softly to myself') of the mysterious words (*paralysis, gnomon, simony*) which leaven the scrupulously naturalistic account of Dublin. The reader is constantly thrown back upon their own interpretative resources to make sense of stories which are both vividly realistic and relentlessly symbolic. They cannot be reduced to a single meaning; they are located in no dominant discourse.

In fifty years of teaching Joyce one of the most memorable moments came early in 1976 in Cambridge. I had just sketched this analysis of *Dubliners* when a young undergraduate rose, an action unheard of in a Cambridge lecture, and read out a sentence describing Mrs Mooney, the landlady in 'The Boarding House': 'She dealt with moral problems as a cleaver deals with meat' (*D*, 47). Was this not a good example of a dominant discourse in which the narrative provided fixed identification? The young undergraduate was Adam Mars-Jones, subsequently a student and friend and currently a grand old man of English letters. He wasn't a grand old man then but he was right.

As I read and reread *Dubliners*, in the light of Mars-Jones's comments, it became clear that there were three stories, 'A Painful

Case', 'The Boarding House', and 'A Mother', which differed significantly from the others. Formally all the other stories could be described geometrically as gnomons, that is to say figures from which a significant element had been removed. It is this excision which renders the stories narratively incomplete and it is this incompleteness which meant that scrupulous naturalistic description could leave room for an undecidability in which the reader was forced into a modernist mode of interpretation. These three stories, although they shared the naturalistic description, were narratively less truncated or doubled. The reader was left less room for analysis. This formal difference is linked to the similar subject matter of the three stories. All have at their centre a mother: Mrs Sinico, Mrs Mooney, Mrs Kearney. Joyce was happy to leave young girls like Eveline and old maids like Maria in a state of narrative indeterminacy, their identities escaping both reader and writer. When it came to the figure of the mother, so central to the Irish imagination at the end of the 19th century, Joyce was compelled to produce a more complete picture which left less for the reader to interpret.

And if he did not do justice to his mothers, he could not do justice to Mother Ireland. Had Grant Richards published *Dubliners* in 1906 and had 'Grace' been the last story of the collection, this weakness might well have been more evident, but the purgatory of Joyce's battles with the moral qualms of British printers meant that he had two years of living with the mother of his children to find a different ending to his collection. In between the original magazine publication of 'The Sisters' in 1904 and the opening story of the collection he sent to Richards in 1905 he had found three words to provide a gloss for his stories. Paralysis provided the most general description of Dublin's inability to live. Gnomon afforded a formal description of Joyce's method of incompleteness. Simony described the corrupt Church which was the subject matter of both the first story 'The Sisters' and the last story 'Grace'. But now there was a fourth word and a new theme: *hospitality*. Joyce wrote to Stanislaus from Rome on 25 September 1906:

'Sometimes thinking of Ireland it seems to me at least that I have been unnecessarily harsh. I have reproduced (in Dubliners at least) none of the attractions of the city for I have never felt at my ease in any city since I left it except in Paris. I have not reproduced its ingenuous insularity and its hospitality. The latter "virtue" so far as I can see does not exist elsewhere in Europe' (*Letters II*, 111).

It is hospitality that dominates the first two-thirds of 'The Dead' as the Misses Morkans' annual Christmas party is described in loving detail. James Joyce is one of the most evocative of food writers and there can be no doubt that his description of the Christmas dinner on Usher Island is his greatest gastronomic moment. At the centre of the dinner is the goose (unfortunately minus apple sauce) that Gabriel carves so expertly and Gabriel Conroy is yet another of the versions of Joyce that populate *Dubliners*. This version of Joyce is both of completely different physical appearance and of very different temperament. One cannot imagine the language teacher of Trieste fussing about his children's diet or his wife's galoshes. Nor does Gabriel Conroy drink much. But like Joyce he writes reviews for the *Daily Express*, like Joyce he is anti-nationalist, and like Joyce he has married a woman of lower social status from the West of Ireland.

The portrait of Mrs Conroy is much more directly drawn from Joyce's wife Nora Barnacle. It is not just that they speak the same idioms and share the same origins, the physical description of Gretta is modelled directly on Nora. More important yet, the story of Michael Furey which dominates the last third of the novella is taken from Nora's life. And it is in this concluding section that Joyce is able to accept a mother whom he cannot define. The crucial moment comes when Gabriel, boiling with frustrated male desire, demands from his wife a narrative account of her relationship with Michael Furey: 'I suppose you were in love with this Michael Furey, Gretta.' Gretta's reply refuses standard English and the story that her husband demands. Instead she uses an Irish idiom to describe an event: 'I was great with him at that time'

(*D*, 173). Gabriel's desire for mastery in both flesh and word is outplayed and he is left to bemoan in rather maudlin fashion the shattering of his masculine narcissism. It is that shattering, the acceptance of the mother as source of both life and death, that allows him to connect to the dead that people the past of his own country. Joyce has not only left Dublin, he has now returned to it and the country of which it is the capital. He has created his imaginary homeland. The next thing he requires is a hero who will become an exile from it.

Chapter 3
A Portrait

In January of 1904 Joyce wrote, in one day, a 3,000-word autobiographical essay, entitled, at his brother Stanislaus's suggestion, 'A Portrait of the Artist'. The text was submitted for publication to the editors of a new journal, *Dana*. The essay is written in a highly aestheticized prose of a kind that is often identified with the name of Walter Pater. But this is a Walter Pater on speed. The essay sketches a life, complete with religious disillusion, romantic love, and visits to brothels, which is recognizably, in retrospect, the life of Stephen Dedalus in the book that bears the variant title *A Portrait of the Artist as a Young Man* and which was published more than a decade later in 1916.

Eglinton, one of the editors of the new magazine, rejected the article on the grounds that 'I can't print what I can't understand' although he also objected to the hero's sexual exploits (*JJ*, 147). Joyce's response was to sit down and begin a long autobiographical novel planned in sixty-three chapters and with the provisional title *Stephen Hero*.

Throughout 1904 and 1905 he worked concurrently on this novel and the stories for *Dubliners*, an astonishing burst of creativity, all the more astonishing in that the short stories and the novel were antithetical in form. While in *Dubliners* Joyce worked at creating a new style which abandoned narrative and identity in favour of a more precise evocation of time and place, *Stephen Hero* is the narrative of an identity—the identity of the writer. If the stories in *Dubliners* resemble the geometrical figure of the gnomon from which a key element has been removed, nothing has been removed from *Stephen Hero*, which attempts total coverage of the young artist and his environment. Some 200 pages of this early draft of what would become *A Portrait* covering Stephen's time at university have survived and were published in 1944, after Joyce's death, as *Stephen Hero*. There can be no doubting the quality of the writing in this fragment. There are any number of set pieces which delight with their intelligence and wit. One might single out the confrontation with the Dean of Studies over Stephen's proposed public paper on drama for a hilarious account of the stupidity of a university run by religion.

There are also passages which mine deeper emotions, most notably the conversation with his anguished mother when confronted with Stephen's loss of faith. However, the writing assumes a fixed and omniscient identity for the writer and it is just this identity which Joyce is deconstructing in his parallel writing in *Dubliners*. There can be little surprise that Joyce abandoned the project and began a totally new book after finishing 'The Dead'. The masculine narcissism which supports the writing position of Stephen, most obvious in the treatment of Emma Clery—'he felt that even that warm ample body could hardly compensate him for her distressing pertness and middle class affectations' (*SH*, 67)—could not survive Gabriel Conroy's encounter with Gretta. It was at that point that he sat down and began the first three chapters of the *Portrait* that we know.

In the fragment of the abandoned draft that we have, perhaps the biggest narrative change is the role played by Ibsen. Briefly mentioned in the published novel he is a, if not the, major character, albeit offstage in *Stephen Hero*. Stephen reflects on him at length from his introduction on page 40: 'It must be said simply and at once that at this time Stephen suffered the most enduring influence of his life.' Subsequently Stephen engages in long conversations about Ibsen with his fellow student McCann and his mother and the text provides a richly comic sketch of his father Simon Dedalus attempting to read the Norwegian playwright.

In *Stephen Hero* Ibsen is offstage, in Joyce's life he was very briefly almost onstage as well. It is unsurprising that in the late 1890s a young modern languages student obsessed by literature would go to the trouble of obtaining Ibsen's plays in translation. It is still astonishing, however, that at the age of 18 he had the skill and commitment to learn Dano-Norwegian and the opportunistic chutzpah to write a substantial essay on Ibsen's new play *When We Dead Awaken* for *The Fortnightly Review*, one of London's most prestigious literary journals. Even more astonishingly, *The Fortnightly Review* published Joyce's offering and Ibsen, with little English, took the effort to work through the review and to ask the editor to pass on his thanks to the author. It is worth remarking on the incredible social reach that Joyce already commanded. His economic conditions were dire: he was housed in some of the worst slums of the entire British Empire. However, the education on which the Catholic Church placed such a premium in a subjugated Ireland meant that he was able to participate in the most sophisticated metropolitan culture from the base of those very slums.

Ibsen is one of the presiding geniuses throughout the original 3,000-word essay and there is a particularly significant allusion in the final overblown paragraph:

> Man and woman, out of you comes the nation that is to come, the lighting of your masses in travail; the competitive order is employed against itself, the aristocracies are supplanted; and amid the general paralysis of an insane society, the confederate will issues in action (*P*, XI).

The reference to the 'general paralysis' of the 'insane' evokes the closing scene of Ibsen's most famous play, *Ghosts*, when Captain Alving's son Oswald awaits the general paralysis of the insane, the final stages of the syphilis which he has inherited from his father. He is attended by his mother, who has concealed her husband's sexual life, and who now must decide when to administer the fatal dose of morphine which Oswald has procured for her against this very moment. Paralysis is the key term for *Dubliners* because it conjures up syphilis (and conjures it up in its very vowels and consonants), the disease which embodies the Victorian hypocrisy about sex which tied women to the strictest standards of chastity while licensing men to frequent prostitutes. In *A Portrait* Joyce focuses on the spiritual effects of visiting brothels but he was more than aware of the physical traces that such visits left. In a letter from Rome to Stanislaus he railed against the Sinn Fein propaganda which pretended that immorality was peculiar to the Anglo-Saxon and the Gael was naturally pure. 'I presume there are very few mortals in Europe who are not in danger of waking one morning and finding themselves syphilitic. The Irish consider England a sink, but if cleanliness be important in this matter, what is Ireland?' (*Letters II*, 192).

When, after finishing 'The Dead', Joyce sat down to rework completely the material from *Stephen Hero* he did not find it easy. There was an early decision to reduce it to five long chapters but Stanislaus recorded in his diary of 15 December that Joyce complained, 'it began at a railway station like most college stories; there were three companions in it, and a sister who dies by way of pathos. He said that it was the old bag of tricks and that a good critic would probably show that he was still struggling...with the stock figures discarded in Europe half a century ago' (*JJ*, 264).

We do not know the details of *A Portrait*'s gestation but it seems possible that the first chapter, which is in many ways the most strikingly original of the whole novel, may have been written very late. Certainly, when Joyce gave the first three chapters to his pupil and friend Ettore Schmitz (who wrote novels under the pseudonym Italo Svevo) in 1909, Schmitz's enthusiastic response was enormously important in Joyce's decision to continue with the novel. But Schmitz explicitly excluded the first chapter from praise, which suggests that it might still have been the 'old bag of tricks'. When the novel was finally published the first chapter was something undeniably very different. Indeed, the opening lines of the text provide a template not just for *A Portrait* but for *Ulysses* and *Finnegans Wake*:

> Once upon a time and a very good time it was there was a moocow coming down along the road and this moocow that was down along the road met a nicens little boy named baby tuckoo…
>
> His father told him that story: his father looked at him through a glass: he had a hairy face.
>
> He was baby tuckoo. The moocow came along the road: The moocow came down the road where Betty Byrne lived: she sold lemon platt.
>
> *O, the wild rose blossoms*
>
> *On the little green place*
>
> He sang that song. That was his song.
>
> *O, the green wothe botheth.*
>
> When you wet the bed, first it is warm then it gets cold. His mother put on the oilsheet. That had the queer smell.
>
> His mother had a nicer smell than his father. She played on the piano the sailor's hornpipe for him to dance. He danced:
>
> *Tralala lala*
>
> *Tralala tralaladdy*
>
> *Tralala lala*
>
> *Tralala lala.* (3)

The book's very opening lines set up an opposition between language as story and song in which we find identity, and language as sound when identity dissolves into the body. The little boy realizes that he is baby tuckoo in his father's story and he also knows that 'O, the wild rose blossoms' is 'his song'; his party piece. But as he falls asleep the language of the waking day dissolves: '*O, the green wothe botheth*', and social identity is left behind for the reality of the body, a body that wets the bed, a body that distinguishes the smell of the mother and which dances to sound which has no sense or meaning at all.

This opposition between the world of paternal narrative which confers social identity and bodily reality which dissolves that identity in the world of the mother will run through all of Joyce's work. And indeed, *A Portrait* is constructed on a dialectic of masculine identity and female disidentification. At the end of both the first and third chapter Stephen claims his place in society first as a rebel making just complaint to the rector Fr Conmee about having been 'wrongly punished' (54) and then as the repentant sinner who has rejoined the Church—'the ciborium had come to him' (158). The second and fourth chapters end with encounters with women which cause Stephen to lose consciousness. Chapter 2 has left the child that protested about injustice; indeed, the incident becomes a figure of fun when John Stanislaus Joyce petitions Fr Conmee for a free place at Belvedere School for his eldest son.

We have plunged into the maelstrom of an adolescence complicated by the father's squandering of his considerable wealth through drink and improvidence. The ending of the chapter finds Stephen encountering a prostitute in the inner city slums where the family now lives. She bends his head to her mouth: 'It was too much for him. He closed his eyes, surrendering himself to her, body and mind, conscious of nothing in the world but the dark pressure of her softly parting lips' (108). A similar if less carnal experience comes at the end of chapter 4 when Stephen has rejected the Church for a second and more conscious time. He finds himself on a beach observing a young girl wading in the sea who becomes the image of life and art: 'His soul was swooning into some new world, fantastic, dim, uncertain as under sea, traversed by cloudy shapes and beings' (187).

Joyce uses two complementary strategies to break with the unified world of *Stephen Hero*. The first is that the five sections are discontinuous, there is no narrative link at all between Stephen's ecstatic swoon on the beach at the end of chapter 4 and the opening scene of chapter 5 which finds him consuming an impoverished breakfast in the squalid setting of the slum dwelling in which the Dedalus family now reside. If this montage is particularly striking, each chapter break operates a similar exercise which removes key elements of the narrative and models the whole book as a geometrical gnomon. More important still is that each of the chapters uses a narrative written in a style appropriate to Stephen's consciousness. From the very first lines, which take an infant perspective, to chapter 5 where Stephen's thoughts achieve a fully adult articulation, we read a story entirely from Stephen's perspective. A third person narration is told entirely from the perspective of an individual consciousness. While what is referred to as free indirect style has a considerable history which includes both Flaubert and Jane Austen, Joyce is the first author to use the technique for a whole book. He also follows the growth of the individual consciousness, and so the individual perspective changes as our protagonist Stephen Dedalus ages. This is obvious from the very first page where the recognition of the storytelling father is told in the language of a 2-year-old while the reflections on wetting the bed are in the language of a 5- or 6-year-old.

A Portrait's style makes reading a constant act of interpretation, particularly in the first chapter where Stephen's infant consciousness reports events which he does not fully understand. It also makes it almost impossible for the reader to make a firm judgement either of the aesthetic discourse which ends the fourth chapter or the philosophical language which occupies much of the fifth. Are we meant to concur with the young aesthetic philosopher or are we meant to reject his overwritten and overwrought youthful egotism? It is a function of free indirect style that such questions are finally unanswerable in terms of the text.

There can be no doubting the strongly autobiographical reality of *A Portrait*. The titanic family row between Church and state which turns the 9-year-old Stephen's first adult Christmas lunch into a bitter lesson about Charles Stewart Parnell testifies to the text's firm anchoring in historical experience. Equally strongly anchored in Joyce's life are the encounter with the prostitute of the second chapter, the sermon on Hell in the third, and the rejection of the Church for the vocation of Art in the fourth. But the isolated sensitive and largely melancholy individual who stalks the pages of *A Portrait* has little to do with 'Sunny Jim', which was his family's nickname for James—the one member of the Joyce family who was bound to be in a good mood. Even more surprising are memories of his schoolfellows at Clongowes and Belvedere, who remember a sociable boy who was keen on sports, particularly cricket and swimming. Perhaps the most surprising contribution to *The Joyce We Knew: Memoirs of Joyce* is from Ivan Fallon who was a fellow pupil of Joyce's at Belvedere. He occurs under his own name in *A Portrait* where he betrays his bourgeois naivety by asking Stephen why he moves houses so often. Fallon was a jock and was to become president of Irish rugby. He offers a very different perspective on Joyce's summer of 1904: 'Joyce asked me to propose him for my own swimming club, Pembroke. If he had become a member, he would have competed in swimming races, but he had left Dublin before I had an opportunity to propose him' (*JWK*, 47).

When he sat down to write *Stephen Hero*, Joyce was committed to an autobiographical novel. When after the experience of *Dubliners* he turned to rework the material which he had first treated in the 1904 essay 'A Portrait of the Artist', he readopted his original title but he added ironic distance with the prepositional phrase 'as a young man'. He added further distance with an epigraph taken from Ovid: *Et ignotas animum dimittit in artes*—'and he turned his mind to unknown arts'. The quotation is taken from Book VIII of Ovid's *Metamorphoses* and describes how Daedalus, the architect of the labyrinth which housed the Minotaur, fashioned wings which would allow him and his son Icarus to escape from their imprisonment in Crete. The meaning of the Latin *artes* (plural of *ars*) is much, much wider than our contemporary 'art', indeed it is doubtful that 'arts' is a good translation of *artes* in this quotation. It could equally well be translated by 'sciences', for Daedalus' project might best be described in terms of engineering and *ars* covered the whole of what we now call science. However, Ovid's description of Daedalus' task is neither in terms of what we would call science or art. Rather the painstaking construction of the artificial wings is described in terms of craftmanship. Craft, like science, is a term covered by the Latin noun.

Thus, in the first two sentences that a reader encounters before reading the novel the term of 'artist' is ironized twice over. In the English title it is stressed that this is not a portrait of the artist as he is but as he was in youth and in the Latin epigraph the historical variability of the term 'art' and its cognates is emphasized. Chapters 1 and 3 ended with assertions of identity, chapters 2 and 4 with swoons out of identity. The end of chapter 5 might be expected to produce a final synthesis but the ending is heavily undercut by the switch from third to first person. Throughout our reading of the novel we have balanced between Stephen's consciousness and objective description, constantly having to interpret what is Stephen's thought and what narrative description. One might expect the novel to end with a final union between narrative and consciousness which would assert Stephen's true artistic identity.

In chapter 5 the portrait of the languages that make up the artist is fleshed out as we follow Stephen through a day which includes a series of conversations, with the dean of students and with a number of his classmates. Suddenly, however, a few pages before the end, the text changes into diary form of which the first entry is a summary of Stephen's conversation with Cranly, which we have just read in the third person. Far from reaching a discursive close we are treated to a montage of random thoughts in the first person which while they complete various narrative threads offer us no overarching conclusion. The patronized Emma Cleary of *Stephen Hero* who has become the anonymized E…C…is encountered for a final time in the street. The entry concludes:

> Yes, I liked her today. A little or much? Don't know. I liked her and it seems a new feeling to me. Then, in that case, all the rest, all that I thought I thought and all that I felt I felt, all the rest before now, in fact…O, give it up, old chap! Sleep it off! (316)

The novel does however end with a paternal identification:

> …I go to encounter for the millionth time the reality of experience and to forge in the smithy of my soul the uncreated conscience of my race.
>
> APRIL 27. Old father, old artificer, stand me now and ever in good stead. (316).

The grandiloquent language of these closing sentences echoes the discourse of art for art's sake which had closed the previous chapter. While the development of the artist is inflected socially by the justification that this will create the 'conscience of the race', that development is understood as a process of paternal identification. Joyce could tolerate this finale because he knew that it was not the end of the story. Stephen's flight is short-lived and his return to Dublin ignominious. Originally Joyce intended to include that return in *A Portrait* but by the time he was finishing the novel it was clear that the period of Stephen's return from Paris after his mother's death was part of a much bigger project. The project was *Ulysses*. The title had come to Joyce in Rome in the same period when he wrote 'The Dead' and it had its basis in a drunken evening in Dublin in 1904 when Joyce had got in a fight from which he had been rescued by a good Samaritan called Hunter. He wrote later to his brother that he had abandoned the short story but by the time he was finishing *A Portrait* he had in mind a huge novel set on a single day which would include all that the aesthetic discourse of *A Portrait* ignored, from the physical body to everyday reality. The dead ends of aestheticism could be left for *Ulysses*.

As Joyce was finishing *A Portrait*, he was, in addition to beginning work on the huge task of *Ulysses*, completing his only surviving play: *Exiles*. As he was writing *Exiles* it may well have seemed to Joyce like the triumphant conclusion of the long apprenticeship of *Stephen Hero* and *A Portrait*. He was finally writing a drama which he had long held out as the supreme literary genre and he was imitating his master Ibsen both in the three-act form and in the topic: contemporary sexual relations. Joyce never gave up on *Exiles*; he may have regarded his youthful poetry as minor but there is every evidence that he felt *Exiles* to be a major play. Unfortunately, almost nobody has been found to agree with him. The one striking admirer of *Exiles* was Harold Pinter, who mounted a very successful production of the play in London in November 1970.

The plot of *Exiles* is simple: Richard Rowan, a writer, together with his common-law wife Bertha and his son Archie have returned from Europe to a Dublin they left a decade before. They have been urged to return by Beatrice Justice and her cousin Robert Hand, both old friends. The opening act makes clear that both Beatrice and Robert have strong sexual reasons to wish for the couple's return, Richard and Beatrice seem on the verge of an affair, which might well have begun if Richard had stayed in Dublin, and Robert and Bertha are even closer to adultery (they kiss on stage). In the end there are no sexual transgressions but not before all four protagonists have laid bare their souls. The play can claim astonishing prescience in playing out one of the central dramas of 20th-century sexual relationships. This is an Ibsenite play but it is written a generation after Ibsen had unmasked the hypocrisy of 19th-century sexual mores. The crucial question for Joyce is infidelity: no relationship should exclude infidelity because of the restriction on personal freedom but infidelity should not be secret and furtive, it must be honest and open and accepted by all parties. The play might work well as a drama of Bloomsbury London or surrealist Paris, but it seems merely comic in Edwardian Dublin. Robert Hand borrows his name from Roberto Prezioso, the editor of one of Trieste's leading newspapers who had set his cap at Nora, but if a womanizing editor is plausible in the Austro-Hungarian empire, he is more than unlikely in Catholic Ireland. Indeed, Robert's account, in the third act of the play, of how instead of sleeping with Bertha he ended up in a nightclub where he picked up a woman whom he pleasured in the back of a cab, reads like poor adolescent fantasy. In one of the letters that he had written to Grant Richards defending *Dubliners* Joyce wrote, 'he is a very bold man who dares to alter in the presentment, still more to deform, whatever he has seen and heard', but *Exiles* is written almost entirely in an imaginary register (*Letters II*, 134). What reality it has is ducked. The second act begins with Robert waiting for Bertha to keep an assignation, but before Bertha arrives Richard appears to tell Robert that Bertha has kept him abreast of every stage of the nascent affair. At the climax of their confrontation they hold hands and it is difficult not to think that the real focus of the play is not the ethics of fidelity but homosexuality.

However, if Joyce is unable to transpose Trieste to Dublin in dramatic form (Robert Hand would need to speak Triestino Italian) he is able to merge the two cities in the epic form of *Ulysses* where homosexual fantasy will be investigated much more directly and where a woman's voice will take the last word away from Stephen.

Chapter 4
Ulysses

> By close-ups of the things around us, by focusing on hidden details of familiar objects, by exploring commonplace milieus under the ingenious guidance of the camera, the film, on the one hand, extends our comprehension of the necessities which rule our lives; on the other hand, it manages to assure us of an immense and unexpected field of action. Our taverns and our metropolitan streets, our offices and furnished rooms, our railroad stations and our factories appeared to have locked us up hopelessly. Then came the film and burst this prison-world asunder by the dynamite of the tenth of a second, so that now, in the midst of its far-flung ruins and debris, we calmly and adventurously go travelling.

Walter Benjamin's description of the cinema could also function as a perfect introduction to Joyce's great novel *Ulysses* which takes eighteen episodes (some of them as long as a short novella) to narrate one day in the life of the city of Dublin. Indeed, Joyce's novel can be thought of as a child of the cinema. Both its form and content owe much to the new medium which Joyce encountered in Trieste. At a simple biographical level Joyce devoted considerable time and energy to setting up the first cinema in Dublin, the Volta, in 1909–10. A typical programme of that time was a series of short films of very different kinds mixing a documentary of contemporary urban life with exotic material from remote countries, a comic skit with a romantic story, a scene from classic literature with the restaging of a famous historical event. This extraordinary mélange of subject matters offers a good introduction to *Ulysses* where both mood and topic can shift from one paragraph to another with a speed for which the only parallel is the very early cinema. However, if it is convincing to think that the content of Joyce's novel owes something to the cinema, it is its form which is best explained by the new and competitive medium.

The novel in the 19th century, typically Balzac or George Eliot, claimed to have discarded form to achieve a direct transcription of reality. This claim was exploded by the cinema, which recorded reality without any intervening consciousness. Aesthetic debates about realism, with which Joyce was very familiar, had already stressed how the author was always imposing a particular selection of reality; the arrival of cinema made it clear that the medium of writing itself was not neutral, certainly not neutral as the camera was. A consciousness of writing as medium is already evident in *Dubliners* and *A Portrait* but in *Ulysses* it becomes one of the major emphases of the text and our voyage through Dublin is a voyage through all the genres and styles of English.

In some ways we can understand the enormity of the task that Joyce had undertaken if we think of *Ulysses* not under the category of art but under the category of science. Joyce is determined to produce a scientific compendium of all the possibilities offered by writing in English. Joyce would not only produce a truly modern hero in a truly modern epic but would produce a science of writing which would take account of the implications of a world in which representation without an intervening consciousness is possible.

To talk about representation in this way is in effect to allow a multiplication of the real in which the new access to reality offered by the cinema liberates the novel to investigate its own powers to produce new and contradictory perspectives. The advent of the cinema makes clear that we cannot simply conceive reality independently of the practices in which it is represented. As media proliferate it becomes impossible to produce the overarching account offered by the 19th-century novel in which there is a reality, there, and its representation, here. Now we must look at the very complicated ways in which reality and representation are produced within different and contradictory practices.

There is, however, a paradox which has obscured these changes. For the early development of the medium of film saw it captured for an aesthetic based on the 19th-century novel, so that not only was its effect on literature not understood but its own potential was largely undeveloped. The thinker who saw this most clearly was André Bazin. He concluded a review of Hitchcock's *Shadow of a Doubt* in the *Écran français* of 3 October 1945, 'Once again we see it proved that if the cinema so rarely achieves the quality of great American literature, it is not because its possibilities of expression are less but only because the cinema draws back before the normal demands of art.' It is one of Bazin's most important themes of the late 1940s that modernist literature had learnt the epistemological lessons of the cinema as technology better than the cinema had, with rare exceptions like Welles and Rossellini where cinema had achieved modernist forms.

There is no writer who learnt these epistemological lessons better than Joyce. *Ulysses* however is not a philosophical exercise. It borrows its structure from Homer's great epic the *Odyssey*, which begins with Odysseus' son Telemachus setting out to find his father and ends with Odysseus finally returning home after ten years' travel and a multitude of adventures to be reunited with his wife Penelope. Joyce's cinematic technique slows down a single day, 16 June 1904, so that it expands to include ten years' worth of adventures. These adventures all occur within the familiar setting of Dublin and abandon traditional notions of the heroic epic to find a new kind of heroism in the ordinary everyday life of the modern city. They also propose a radical redefinition of masculinity which repudiates simple binary oppositions between the sexes. These questions of heroism and masculinity were not abstract considerations. *Ulysses* was largely written in the shelter of neutral Switzerland as Europe committed suicide in the bloodbath of the First World War. It was completed in Paris as

Ireland engaged in a savage war of independence which would morph into an even more savage civil war. Both European bloodbath and Irish savagery were sustained by the conventional notions of heroism and masculinity, notions that Joyce's novel judges as irredeemably toxic.

For Benjamin film freed us from the prison house of the city by the 'dynamite of the tenth of the second'. Joyce used a wide variety of strategies to slow the city down so that it could become a playground rather than a jail. The first was to limit the time of the novel to one day in the life of the city. At a stroke almost all plot devices which depend on the passage of time are abolished. Instead of plotting the ordering of the material is determined by the passage of time from early morning till late at night. *Ulysses* is a record of one day (16 June 1904) largely from the perspectives of three characters, Stephen Dedalus, Leopold Bloom, and Molly Bloom. Their paths cross when late at night Stephen is abandoned by his witty and malicious friends and Bloom rescues him from a fight with soldiers outside a brothel. He then takes him home for a reviving cup of chocolate. After Bloom falls asleep, his wife Molly meditates on her life.

From his brief correspondence with his brother when he first considered Ulysses as a short story for a second volume of *Dubliners* in 1907, the strategy of limiting the action to one day was linked to a further structure—the voyages of Ulysses. In choosing Ulysses as the symbolic double for a Dubliner Joyce had given himself a structure which would further impede any simple narrative drift. Each chapter (there would be eighteen in all) would be modelled on one of the famous adventures of the Greek hero Odysseus, although Joyce did not use the Greek name. Joyce first encountered Odysseus and the ten years that it took him to sail back from Troy not in the pages of Homer but in Charles Lamb's best-selling novelization *The Adventures of Ulysses*. It was the Latinate Ulysses that Joyce used as the title for the projected short story which morphed into a mammoth epic.

It is close to impossible to calculate the importance of Homer's text. Joyce considered it the key to the book. Both Stuart Gilbert and Frank Budgen, who wrote early books on *Ulysses* based on long discussion with Joyce, stress how obsessed he was by Homeric scholarship. However, there is no indication that Joyce tried to seriously model his text on the Homeric source. Joyce does not follow religiously the order of the episodes and one of the episodes (chapter 10, The Wandering Rocks) relies just on a couple of lines in Homer and the closing episode (chapter 18, Penelope) has no direct parallel at all in the classical text. Some idea of how Homer functioned for Joyce can be seen in a letter he wrote to Budgen as he was finishing the longest and most experimental chapter: Circe. In Homer Odysseus is able to avoid the fate of his men, who have been turned into pigs, by using an antidote to Circe's poison. The antidote is a plant named moly which has been given to him by the god Hermes. There is a rich classical scholarship trying to identify this plant. Here's Joyce's effort in a letter to Budgen dated Michaelmas 1920:

> Moly is the nut to crack. My latest is this. Moly is the gift of
> Hermes, god of public ways and is the invisible influence (prayer,
> chance, agility, presence of mind, power of recuperation) which
> saves in case of accident. This would cover immunity from syphilis
> (σύ φιλος = swinelove?). Hermes is the god of signposts: he is,
> specially for a traveler like Ulysses, the point at which roads
> parallel merge and roads contrary also. He is an accident of
> Providence. In this case the plant may be said to have many leaves,
> indifference due to masturbation, pessimism congenital, a sense of
> the ridiculous, sudden fastidiousness in some detail,
> experience. (*Letters I*, 147–8)

The letter is typical of Joyce's whole writing procedure by 1920. An interpretation is promised but immediately multiplies into an indefinite list aided by etymologies which play with the material of language but have little basis in historical reality. Homer's text is not used by Joyce to provide an allegorical key to *Ulysses* but as a new and powerful strategy to complicate and problematize narrative. From his very first writings Joyce had resisted narrative and the unveiling of psychological identity that it promises. For Joyce identity does not reside in a non-existent psychology but in the repetitions of the everyday. Homer offers one method to access this everyday by doubling the narrative and refusing any single identity.

Thus in the opening chapters of *Ulysses* Stephen Dedalus is the young man whose life we have followed in *A Portrait* but he is also Telemachus, Odysseus' son who, sickened and disgusted by the suitors who besiege his mother Penelope, decides that he will set out to discover what has happened to his father, now absent for twenty years. The suitors are represented by Buck Mulligan, a silver-tongued master of language, and his Oxford friend Haines, a walking chapter of clichés, who is visiting Ireland as a cultural tourist. Mulligan is a hypocritical toady who denigrates Haines as English behind his back. However, when the old woman who supplies them with fresh milk arrives Mulligan uses academic English in order to talk to Haines about the old woman without her understanding what is said.

This unpleasant comedy of exclusive language now becomes savage farce as Haines addresses the woman in a language which is given no phonetic rendering at all. Stephen asks the woman if she understands what is being said and she surmises that Haines is speaking in French. When Mulligan tells the milkwoman it is Irish, she asks Haines if he is from the west—the only part of Ireland in which Gaelic is still spoken. Mulligan corrects her '—He's English and he thinks we ought to speak Irish in Ireland.—Sure, we ought to, the old woman said, and I'm ashamed that I don't speak the language myself. I'm told it's a grand language by them that knows' (16).

This brief linguistic interlude dramatizes Stephen's cultural dilemma. The Gaelic revival, which has attracted Haines's attention, argues that Gaelic, killed over three centuries by brutal English policy, must be brought back to life for Ireland to express the truths of its peasant wisdom. But the urban Stephen is neither a peasant nor an Irish speaker and he is acutely aware of the enormous aesthetic and intellectual resources of the English spoken in Dublin, the language that he and the old woman share and which he will transcribe with relish. Mulligan and Haines, like Penelope's suitors, want to steal and devalue his inheritance. He, like Telemachus, must find some way to rescue his patrimony.

The difficulties of this task are demonstrated in the second chapter which finds Stephen at the school where he has been teaching for the last three months. As with *A Portrait* the break between the end of one chapter and the beginning of another stresses discontinuity. Even this story of one day in Dublin will make no attempt to a comprehensive representation, it is a gnomon, a figure produced by excision. We are given no hint as to how Stephen got to the school or what precedes the discussion of Pyrrhus' defeat at Asculum. What the beginning of the chapter does make clear is that Stephen has little time for the formal transmission of knowledge. Half-remembered dates and names and poetry read without comprehension do not keep his attention which returns, as it already has in chapter 1, to his dead mother. 'She was no more: the trembling skeleton of a twig burnt in the fire, an odour of rosewood and wetted ashes. She had saved him from being trampled under foot and had gone, scarcely having been' (33).

The ghost of his mother haunts Stephen throughout the book until she is exorcized in the hallucinations of the Circe chapter. However, the major focus of this chapter is the lecture on Irish history that the headmaster, Garret Deasy, delivers to Stephen as he pays him his month's wages after he has finished teaching and while the boys are playing hockey. Deasy's model in the *Odyssey* is Nestor, one of the heroes of Troy to whom Telemachus goes for advice as to how to find his father. Even in Homer Nestor is given to pomposity but his wisdom goes unquestioned. Deasy is not only pompous but a fount of misinformation. He attempts to minimize the lethal hostility of protestants for Catholics in the history of Ireland, to condemn the sexual transgressions of women for the tragedies of Irish history, and to blame the Jews for England's decline. Stephen dissents either silently or politely from this stream of bigotry. One of his most quoted responses is to Deasy's Hegelian claim that

> All history moves towards one great goal, the manifestation of God.
>
> Stephen jerked his thumb towards the window, saying:
>
> —That is God.
>
> Hooray! Ay! Whrrwhee!
>
> —What? Mr Deasy asked.
>
> —A shout in the street, Stephen answered, shrugging his shoulders. (42)

Stephen rejects all those claims to turn history into meaning because they all paralyse him into frozen identities: a British subject, a Roman Catholic, an Irish nationalist. Stephen prefers sound to sense: the cries of the boys playing hockey are the raw material from which meaning can be fashioned. This process, which is the process of *Ulysses* itself, is where we can locate the divine, not in a transcendent God but in the earthly transformations of language.

The impersonation of wise Nestor by bigoted Deasy makes it impossible to understand Homer's *Odyssey* as a simple model for Joyce's *Ulysses*. It is possible to argue that Deasy is meant to represent the failure of traditional authority in Joyce's Dublin, but this, like Joyce's letter to Budgen, opens up a vertiginous series of interpretations. The *Odyssey* does not function as classical allegory by one-to-one correspondence, instead it is a device for producing multiple identities. This is even clearer in the third chapter which is usually referred to as Proteus. Joyce gave each of his chapters a name drawn from the *Odyssey*. The early prepublication in *The Little Review* used these names as titles and indeed they were long intended to appear in the book as chapter headings. It was not until late in the publication process that they were dropped. However, for all dedicated readers of Joyce the chapters are referred to by these Homeric titles. Telemachus does not encounter Proteus directly. Nestor has no news of Odysseus but directs Telemachus to Sparta, whose King Menelaus may be better informed. Menelaus does have information that he had extracted from Proteus when he was becalmed in Egypt on his way home from Troy. Proteus, the old man of the sea, will only give up his secrets when he has been captured, a task made exceptionally difficult by his ability to constantly and variously change shape and appearance. Menelaus ignores this shape shifting and, having captured Proteus, makes him speak. One piece of information he divulges is that Odysseus is a prisoner of the nymph Calypso.

Deasy is an incongruous fit for Nestor but as Stephen walks alone on Sandymount Strand there is no direct correspondence at all for Proteus. Stephen opens the chapter by reflecting on the relation between the world and our sensual perception of it and it is reality itself which becomes protean as Stephen experiments with his senses and the world appears and disappears. The protean nature of reality is emphasized by the fact that the whole of the chapter is dominated by Stephen's stream of consciousness.

In *A Portrait* Joyce had used the indirect free style where all third person sentences are from a particular point of view. The opening chapters of *Ulysses* go one stage further. The third person is dropped but it is not replaced by first person statements but by a jumble of subjective thoughts, some direct perception, some memory, some quotation. It has been the dominant style of the first two chapters but both chapters contain some third person description and interruptions by Mulligan, Haines, and Deasy. In Proteus there are no other speakers and Stephen's continuous stream of consciousness needs constant rereading to yield its rich harvest of meaning.

It is paradoxically true that *Ulysses* can only be reread and it is in Proteus that this rereading becomes essential. A good example comes early in the walk along the beach when Stephen thinks that he will visit his uncle Richie Goulding and his aunt Sara. There is a page-and-a-half description of the visit and it is only after a further two-page digression that we read, 'I have passed the way to Aunt Sara's. Am I not going there?' (50–1). It is only at that point that we can read back and discover that the digressions are not part of the visit, which only occurred in anticipation, and that the digressions had made Stephen miss the turning that would have made the visit actual.

There is a moment when Proteus is invoked directly in the chapter but it is not as a character. Stephen encounters two cocklepickers with a dog. In a long passage as the dog runs along the beach he is described in terms of other animals: a hare, a deer, a bear, a wolf, a calf (57–8). Homer's *Odyssey* is so useful to Joyce not only because it complicates narrative and identity but also because it can be used to multiply linguistic choices. Joyce combines a fierce allegiance to reality with a hyperconscious awareness of the variety of linguistic choices available to render that reality. He is always looking for strategies that detach those choices from any univocal narrative. Homer is throughout the most important but Shakespeare is also a continual reference. In addition, each chapter is allocated an organ of the body, a colour, and a technique. Much early criticism of Joyce, much of it dictated by the master himself, emphasized these complicated schemas but, as with Homer, it is better to understand them not in a positive sense but as ways of avoiding a simple narrative which resolves the characters into fixed identities or a straightforward description which renders reality univocal.

As he was beginning Proteus and before leaving Trieste for Zurich, Joyce wrote to Pound on 30 June 1915 to describe his new book:

'It is a continuation of *A Portrait of the Artist as a Young Man* after three years interval blended with many of the persons of *Dubliners*' (*JJ*, 383). It is perhaps wise that Joyce did not alert the anti-Semitic Pound that the book's major character was a Jew whose forebears came from the Austro-Hungarian empire in which Joyce had lived for almost all of the decade after he left Dublin in 1904. Largely landlocked, the Dual Monarchy, as it was often called, had only one port—the city of Trieste, and this made Trieste one of the most important trading cities of the Mediterranean.

Its geographical position ensured it had a hugely mixed population. In addition to the majority Italians it had large numbers of Slovenians and Austrians and a significant Greek presence. It also had a large Jewish population and many of Joyce's friends were Jews. Indeed, he fell in love with one of his Jewish students, Amelia Popper, and made a record of his teacher's crush in a prose poem ironically entitled *Giacomo Joyce*, Giacomo not only being the Italian for James but also the Christian name of the legendary lover Casanova. There is nothing legendary about Joyce's lovemaking; the entirely chaste affair is a question of looks, glances, and heavily coded dialogue. Joyce finished the prose poem around 1913 in the astonishing burst of creativity which saw him finish *A Portrait*, write *Exiles*, and begin the first three chapters of *Ulysses*. *Giacomo Joyce* was not published until nearly thirty years after Joyce's death but, unlike his poetry, which is anaemic at best, this prose poem, to which the loved one's Jewishness is central, is a minor masterpiece.

Another Triestino from whom he sought out information about Jewish customs and ritual was his pupil Ettore Schmitz, a successful businessman with a Christian wife. Joyce took Schmitz into his most intimate confidence when in 1909, disheartened by his battles over the publication of *Dubliners* and unable to see how to finish *A Portrait*, he gave Schmitz the three chapters he had completed to ask his opinion. He was delighted with Schmitz's positive responses and one can speculate that these conversations are one of the deep roots of Bloom and Stephen's encounter at the end of *Ulysses*. He certainly gave Leopold Bloom many of Schmitz's characteristics, not least his delight in offal, with which the fourth chapter introduces our modern Ulysses (it is worth noting that Joyce loathed offal): 'Mr. Leopold Bloom ate with relish the inner organs of beasts and fowls. He liked thick giblet soup, nutty gizzards, a stuffed roast heart, liver slices fried with crustcrumbs, fried hencod's roes. Most of all he liked grilled mutton kidneys which gave to his palate a fine tang of faintly scented urine' (65).

As readers we know Stephen Dedalus well. The first three chapters of *Ulysses* could be published as the final three chapters of an enlarged *Portrait* as, indeed, they were first intended. However, Leopold Bloom is unknown to us and the first three chapters introduce us to our epic protagonist. To track each narrative and biographical strand of these chapters would be to produce a book nearly the length of *Ulysses*. From this first chapter, which is meant to parallel Ulysses' seven years' imprisonment by the nymph Calypso and thus awards Molly Bloom two Homeric identities—she is both the alluring nymph Calypso in this episode and the faithful wife Penelope in the final chapter—we can pick out two very different threads.

The first is a constant emphasis of the book, the appointment which will bring Blazes Boylan, the musical impresario, to 7 Eccles Street at 4 p.m. to discuss an upcoming concert tour with Molly, who is to be the star of the show. Bloom is in little doubt that the discussions will end in adultery. In writing a modern epic Joyce was above all determined to redefine classical heroism, 'whose whole structure is, and always was, a damned lie' as he wrote to Stanislaus in 1905 when he was contemplating the story 'Two Gallants' (*Letters II*, 80). Neither Stephen nor Bloom is any kind of physical hero and if this bothers Stephen, it is of no concern to

Bloom. However, Bloom does enjoy contemporary heroic status, in his refusal to make any attempt to hinder the adultery of his wife.

The theme which stumbles lamely in *Exiles* is triumphantly achieved in *Ulysses* where Bloom's determination not to infringe his wife's liberty is countersigned by the homosexual pleasure which the assignation affords his unconscious. That pleasure will be triggered towards the end of the book as Bloom loses the potato which, in the opening chapter of the book, makes a minor appearance as his lucky charm: 'On the doorstep he felt in his hip pocket for the latchkey. Not there. In the trousers I left off. Must get it. Potato I have' (67). These few sentences set up both Bloom's need to climb into his own house in the penultimate chapter, Ithaca (because he forgets to remember his key), and also the loss of the potato in the brothel in Circe which triggers a series of bisexual fantasies. This short passage is a good example of how the briefest of sentences in Ulysses are charged with multiple narrative meanings and that these meanings are often unavailable on a first reading of the book.

Joyce had promised Pound 'many of the persons of Dubliners' but none had appeared in the first four chapters. However, from chapter 5 onwards they swarm on to the page. As Bloom sets out from his house, he is accosted by C. P. M'Coy, a character in 'Grace'. Later he bumps into Bantam Lyons, a mere name in 'Ivy Day in the Committee Room' but an important figure in the narrative of *Ulysses*. Lyons wants to borrow Bloom's paper so he can check the runners and riders in the Gold Cup. Bloom says that he can keep the paper as he was about to throw it away. Lyons, totally fixated on betting on the race, hears the comment as a tip to back the rank outsider Throwaway and it is this misunderstanding which later in the day persuades all the drinkers in Barney Kiernan's that Bloom has won a fortune when Throwaway gallops off with the race.

Chapter 5 models itself on Odysseus' encounter with the Lotus Eaters, who offer a narcotic flower which robs the eater of both memory and energy. Much of the chapter is taken up with Bloom's view of religion, which is resolutely negative. Born to a Jewish father who had converted to the protestant Church of Ireland and having himself converted from that Church to Catholicism in order to marry his wife, Bloom has sampled religions widely but he is resolutely sceptical and secular. He has none of Stephen's obsession with theology; his reflections on the Mass he observes are sociological and anthropological. The host that the Dublin congregation swallow is an obvious parallel to the lotus flower which renders Odysseus' men without energy.

One of the most famous episodes in the *Odyssey* is the journey to the underworld where Odysseus talks to the dead. Bloom's parallel journey in the sixth chapter has nothing supernatural about it. He is one of the mourners accompanying his friend Paddy Dignam to be buried in Glasnevin cemetery. The carriage in which he travels is full of familiar faces—Simon Dedalus from *A Portrait*, Martin Cunningham and Jack Power from 'Grace'. Bloom's interior monologue, an alternative name for stream of consciousness, provides a running commentary on the funeral largely concerned with his reflections on death.

We are now used to Bloom's train of thought. His sentences are shorter than Stephen's and very little concerned with the Western tradition either literary or religious. His cast of mind is scientific, always seeking for a materialist explanation of the phenomena that catch his eye, although his schoolboy science is not always sufficient for the task at hand. He is endlessly curious and despite his troubles—the suicide of his father, Molly's likely adultery, his son dead at eleven days—he is a buoyant character and takes pleasure from every encounter. While no one is actively rude to him, he is not greeted warmly, or automatically included in conversation. Indeed, the further we read through the book the more we realize that Bloom is a deliberate outsider to the world of

Dubliners; he is not a Catholic, and he neither drinks nor gambles: the two fundamental bonds of Dublin's homosocial world.

In the first six chapters, it is first Stephen's and then Bloom's stream of consciousness which provides a centre to the text. With the seventh chapter, Aeolus, named after the Homeric god of the winds, we participate in both Bloom's and Stephen's stream of consciousness but neither is central. Instead the chapter focuses on writing as each section is prefaced by a tabloid headline and the reader has to move back and forth to understand the relation of headline to text. There has been a lot of reading and rereading already in the first six chapters but in these earlier cases the second reading merely expands the first, as in the letters, Deasy's, Milly's, Martha's, that punctuate the narrative.

In the offices of the *Freeman's Journal*, as the doors bang open and shut and the assembled hacks expel hot air, the repetition is of a very different order. The newspaper headlines and the text that expands them are written in very different discourses. This not only provides some excellent jokes but it also makes the question of writing and interpretation central to the chapter. Indeed, from this chapter on *Ulysses* becomes more and more attentive to its own construction. A striking example comes just before J. J. O'Molloy quotes from a famous legal case. The text reads 'False lull. Something quite ordinary' (177). This is recognizably Stephen's inner thought. The sentence which follows, 'Messenger took out his matchbox thoughtfully and lit his cigar', is closer to a third person description but the ellipsis of the definite article before 'Messenger' marks it stylistically as Stephen's thought (177). However we then read a startlingly inelegant sentence which is much more difficult to place: '**I have often thought since on looking back over that strange time that it was that small act, trivial in itself, that striking of that match, that determined the whole aftercourse of both our lives**' (177; my emphasis).

The sentence contains the word 'that' no fewer than six times. Four of those occurrences are as a demonstrative pronoun which attempts to specify the event to which the sentence attributes such importance: '**that** strange time...**that** small act...**that** striking of **that** match'. However, as each 'that' increases the power of language as microscope, reality disappears in a puff of smoke. The naturalist critique of realism was that the realist novel operated too selective and too subjective a description of reality and that by more objective procedures naturalism would include elements of both sex and class which realism ignored. Joyce was much influenced by this naturalist critique but this sentence demonstrates how naturalism founders on the fact that there is no procedure which can bring the description of reality to an agreed conclusion. If the cascade of demonstratives ruins the naturalist project, the final 'that' which introduces a relative clause, '**that** determined the whole aftercourse of both our lives', mocks the pretensions of realism to isolate significant events within a life. The microscope of the demonstratives which renders reality ever more specific is counterposed to the telescope of the relative clause which contains no specificity whatsoever. This inelegant sentence provides an elegant critique of the traditional structure of the novel. It offers both a description of an event and its significance in a life, but ruins both event and significance.

The sixth use of 'that' subordinates both event and significance to the reflections of a subject: '**I** have often thought...**that** it was that small act...'. The difficulty for the reader is to identify this **I**. Is this Stephen Dedalus looking forward to the book that he will write or James Joyce looking back to the book he is writing? Nor is this difficulty easily resolved. We can imagine Stephen listening to the journalistic blowhards and amusing himself by turning the scene into a novelistic form. However we can also imagine Joyce determined to demonstrate the kind of novel he is not writing by mimicking a sentence form that Dickens uses in both *David Copperfield* and *Great Expectations* (*UA*, 146). Indeed it is in this seventh chapter of the book that the complex dialectic whereby

Joyce is writing Stephen in order to become Joyce begins to manifest itself. Joyce's writing becomes part of the texture of *Ulysses* in the Aeolus chapter. More characters from *Dubliners* appear (Gabriel Conroy is mentioned on page 159). Indeed, Stephen's parable of the plums that ends the chapter reads like an offcut from *Dubliners*.

Stephen and Bloom's paths cross in the newspaper office but they do not meet. While the blowhards of Dublin compare oratory in the editor's office Bloom is trying to negotiate the placing of an advertisement. The next chapter starts as he makes his leisurely way to the national library to find an example of the design for the ad in a local newspaper. It is lunchtime and Bloom's thoughts are shot through with eating and food. The chapter is called the Lestrygonians after the cannibals who devour many of Odysseus' companions and it includes one of the most disgusting descriptions of eating ever written. Bloom has planned to have lunch at the Burton but as he enters the restaurant he is nauseated and repulsed by a roomful of men slobbering over their food. He decides instead to have a quick snack at Davy Byrne's pub where there is desultory conversation about horses and the Gold Cup. The chapter gives us an enormous amount of information about Bloom's past life. Two dominant strands run through Bloom's wide-ranging memories and reflections. The first is the death of his son Rudy more than a decade before after only eleven days of life. The other is the meeting set for 4 p.m. between Molly and Blazes Boylan at 7 Eccles Street. He has already glimpsed Boylan in the Hades chapter but now, after he leaves Davy Byrne's pub, Bloom sees him fast approaching and he avoids a direct confrontation by quickly ducking into the national museum.

The national museum is opposite the national library and it is in the library that Stephen is voicing his interpretation of Shakespeare. *Voice* is here the exact verb: Stephen's whole emphasis is on speech, on a performance that will both wrest a meaning from Shakespeare and confer an identity on himself within the Irish literary movement. Stephen's theory which identifies Shakespeare not with the Prince but with his dead father—the Ghost of Act I—uses the biographical methods of then current literary criticism. But while Stephen confronts a text, Joyce addresses the context of the critical act itself, the interplay between speech and action in the library. What comes into focus as a result is the very act of writing that displaces the presumed centrality of speech. Early in the chapter, which enjoys the Homeric title of Scylla and Charybdis, John Eglinton, one of Stephen's small band of auditors, attempts to dismiss the importance of Ann Hathaway, who Stephen argues cuckolded Shakespeare:

—The world believes that Shakespeare made a mistake, he said, and got out of it as quickly and as best he could.

—Bosh! Stephen said rudely. A man of genius makes no mistakes. His errors are volitional and are the portals of discovery.   (243)

Stephen's speech is violent but Joyce's writing is comic. The next sentence in the text reads:

Portals of discovery opened to let in the quaker librarian, softcreakfooted, bald, eared and assiduous.   (243)

The repetition of portals of discovery draws attention to the written nature of the text we are reading and achieves its comic effect by transposing Stephen's grandiloquent formulation to the banal opening and shutting of the library doors.

As Stephen sits in the library trying to create both Shakespeare and himself at the centre of the world, the library doors open and close, beyond his control, producing elements which constantly remake his world. As the chapter closes Bloom and Stephen will pass through the doors together but Stephen is still unable to embrace the chance encounters which will remake him.

It is, however, clear by the end of the chapter that Shakespeare cannot serve as a model for Joyce. For Stephen, Shakespeare is intimately involved in the new property relations that are so crucial to capitalism and these new property relations intensify sexual possessiveness: '...a man who holds so tightly to what he calls his rights over what he calls his debts will hold tightly also to what he calls his rights over her whom he calls his wife' (264). Shakespeare's symbolic solution to adulterous wives is the pure daughters of the late plays who have renounced all sexuality. This is not a solution that a disciple of Ibsen can accept. And Shakespeare is no more acceptable politically than sexually. Scylla and Charybdis ends with a quotation from *Cymbeline* whose heroine Imogen is 'as chaste as unsunned snow'. This late play weaves together the murderous jealousy of her husband Posthumus, who has been fooled into thinking her unfaithful by Iachimo, with a political narrative that opposes Britain to the dominant Roman Empire. The conclusion, which includes Britain within the *pax Romana* and reveals Imogen as sexually innocent, bears witness to the sexual and political repressions that underpin Shakespeare's Utopian vision. *Cymbeline* is particularly significant because it contains forty-seven of Shakespeare's forty-eight uses of the word Britain. All the previous history plays have concerned themselves with England but *Cymbeline* is written after James VI of Scotland had acceded to the throne of England in 1603 and is concerned with a polity that both includes a Celtic periphery and acknowledges Roman dominance.

Right at the end of the Scylla and Charybdis chapter and before referring to *Cymbeline* Stephen thinks, 'Cease to strive' (280). Although this is not a direct quotation from the play it refers to the end of the play when King Cymbeline urges Iachimo to 'Strive, man, and speak'. In ceasing to strive Stephen is abandoning speech and it is the abandonment of speech that allows the chapter to be written. It is by repressing the desire to speak a truth so final that it will freeze speaker and audience in their place that Stephen can prepare the way for a writing that will open up multiple identities. In the course of the chapter Joyce plays with repetition, dramatization, and the decomposition of words to emphasize the written nature of the text we are reading. All of these have been foreshadowed in the newspaper office, but they now become a major focus of the text. One of the most striking examples of form becoming meaning and a vivid demonstration of Joyce's virtuosity as a writer comes at the end of a passage when he reflects on the debt that he owes to A. E. Russell and produces the standard order of the vowels as a meaningful sequence: 'A.E.I.O.U.' (243)

A crucial element in the move from frozen speech to fluid writing is the laughter that erupts at the end of Stephen's performance when he concludes a catalogue of examples from Shakespeare's plays 'and in all the other plays that I have not read' and then laughs 'to free his mind from his mind's bondage' (272). Throughout the second half of the chapter Stephen is interrupted and irritated by Buck Mulligan with his non-stop fluent witticisms. Mulligan's wisecracks are fully understood jests that in no way threaten his basic speaking voice, in fact they confirm the centrality of speech. Stephen's joke about the content of plays that he has not read deploys a more subversive irony that eats away at the dominance of the voice that is striving for a total interpretation.

The novel's shift from speech to writing was more strongly marked in manuscript than in the published book. The manuscript that Joyce sold to the New York lawyer John Quinn has a note at the end of Scylla and Charybdis: 'End of first part of *Ulysses*'.

Scylla and Charybdis in Homer names a dangerous sea passage between a six-headed man-eating monster Scylla and a deadly whirlpool Charybdis. Odysseus is advised to take this route by Circe because the alternative, a stretch of sea which is populated by ever-clashing rocks, is even more perilous. Joyce navigated where Homer did not dare to sail and a couple of lines that describe this hazard in the *Odyssey* burgeon into a full chapter, The Wandering Rocks, in *Ulysses*.

Scylla and Charybdis ends with the opening lines of the final speech in *Cymbeline*:

> Laud we the gods
> And let our crooked smokes climb to their nostrils
> From our bless'd altars. (280)

Joyce ends the quotation there but the succeeding lines are an almost perfect introduction to the next episode:

> Publish we this peace
> To all our subjects. Set we forward: let
> A Roman and a British ensign wave
> Friendly together: so through Lud's-town march.

It is Dublin rather than London (Lud's town) through which we march in this episode, but the episode is bookended by Fr Conmee at the beginning and a viceregal cavalcade at the end representing the powers of Rome and Britain which hold Dublin in their tyrannical grip. In between these two vignettes there are a further seventeen short episodes. Bloom features in one and Stephen in two but we also encounter a host of Dubliners both familiar, such as Lenehan, and unfamiliar, such as Paddy Dignam's son. At first glance the episode might read as the apogee of Joyce's naturalistic depiction of Dublin with which we have been familiar since *Dubliners* but each vignette is interrupted by sentences from other vignettes that are not integrated into the host narrative. These interruptions emphasize that we are dealing with a set of synchronous events, but they also draw attention to the different perspectives that make up the chapter. This is cubist naturalism.

The multiplication of perspectives emphasizes the limitations of naturalism but the episodes themselves exhibit Joyce's extraordinary mastery of what has been his chosen form since his first stories in *Dubliners*. The chapter also weaves a multitude of existing narrative threads into a more complex cloth. Paddy Dignam is one such thread. It is Dignam's funeral that pervades Bloom's thoughts in the morning and it is Bloom's efforts to help his widow which will bring him both to Barney Kiernan's pub and a violent altercation with the Citizen and to Sandymount Strand and his sexual encounter with Gerty McDowell. Dignam's wife does not appear as a character in the novel but the penultimate episode of The Wandering Rocks introduces us to Master Patrick Aloysius Dignam as he runs an errand for his mother. He is pleased to get out of the house but his enjoyment of Dublin's streets is marred by his collar stud: 'His collar sprang up again and he tugged it down. The blooming stud was too small for the buttonhole of the shirt, blooming end to it' (323). The final sentences skirt sentimentality while evoking real pathos:

James Joyce

> Pa is dead. My father is dead. He told me to be a good son to ma. I couldn't hear the other things he said but I saw his tongue and his teeth trying to say it better. Poor pa. That was Mr Dignam, my father. I hope he is in purgatory now because he went to confession to father Conroy on Saturday night. (324)

The chapter marks Joyce's envoi to the naturalist method and it also is his farewell to the most striking creation of that method: Stephen Dedalus. Stephen will continue to be a major character in the final chapters in *Ulysses* and we will observe his actions and hear his words. However, the extraordinary textual intimacy bestowed from the indirect free style of the opening page of *A Portrait* to the stream of consciousness of the library chapter in *Ulysses* is coming to an end.

Our final moments of intimacy focus on Stephen Dedalus' sisters. The date of the action of the novel (16 June 1904) is revealed when Blazes Boylan's secretary types out a letter in the middle of the chapter. Five months later Joyce would leave Dublin for a life in Europe, foreshadowed by the Italian that dominates Stephen's first appearance in this chapter when he talks with his teacher Almidano Artifoni. There can be little doubt that Joyce was delighted to bid farewell to both Roman Catholic Church and British Empire. Mulligan has from the opening page of the novel represented literary Dublin and the vignette in this chapter where Mulligan demonstrates real malevolence towards Stephen confirms that the world of Irish letters was equally repellent to him. However, he was also leaving a houseful of young sisters to a life of poverty and a drunken and feckless father. The heartbreaking scene where he meets Dilly Dedalus buying a French primer with one of the two pennies that she had scrounged from their father leaves us in no doubt that he is abandoning responsibility for his sisters:

> She is drowning. Agenbite. Save her. Agenbite. All against us. She will drown me with her, eyes and hair. Lank coils of seaweed hair around me, my heart, my soul. Salt green death.
>
> We.
>
> Agenbite of inwit. Inwit's agenbite.
>
> Misery! Misery!   (313)

Agenbite of inwit is one of the key phrases of *Ulysses*. It flashes through Stephen's mind in the opening chapter (18–19) and again in the Library sequence (243, 313). It is Middle English and uses entirely words derived from the Germanic Anglo-Saxon, literally the 'biting again of the interior mind'. In current English it is translated as 'remorse of conscience', both nouns derived from French and Latin. It is this remorse about his mother's death which is what Stephen must free himself from in order to leave his youth and Ireland behind. It attacks with enormous power when he encounters his sister because his mother's greatest anxiety on her deathbed was who would look after her motherless daughters.

As the novel leaves Stephen and the world of speech behind, its focus shifts decisively to writing. The next chapter opens with two pages of truncated words or phrases that make no coherent sense. Fifty-seven of these fifty-eight phrases and words are repeated in the course of the chapter and gain meanings as they reappear within fuller verbal contexts. The fifty-seventh entry is a single word 'Done' which will also end the chapter, and the fifty-eighth entry, that is not repeated in the body of the text, is 'Begin!' The chapter emphasizes both the material basis of language and that meaning is produced across time by a process of deferred interpretation.

The primary opposition in the chapter is between the bar of the Ormond hotel in which a group of men, of whom the most important is Simon Dedalus, flirt with the barmaids and sing sentimental songs, and the restaurant of the hotel where Bloom is eating a late lunch and writing a letter to his erotic penpal Martha Clifford. While the men in the bar bathe in masculine narcissism, their phallic identity confirmed by the simpering barmaids, Bloom moves between identities as he composes a letter that will be signed Henry Flower and is marked materially by his use of Greek e's as a disguise. The emphasis on the materiality of the letter draws attention to the reader's engagement in the text. The novel does not possess a discrete meaning that can be consumed but offers material that the reader activates with their own meanings. One of the many metaphors for this in the text is the shell that one of the barmaids has brought back from her seaside holiday. The men in the bar think that the sound of the sea is located within the shell while Bloom knows that they are listening to the sound of their circulation: 'The sea they think they hear. Singing. A roar. The blood is it. Souse in the ear sometimes' (363).

This chapter parallels one of the most famous of Odysseus' adventures. Circe warns him that he will sail past the Sirens, fabulous female creatures who sing the most entrancing of songs. The songs lead not to beauty but to certain death, witnessed by the mound of putrid bones on which the Sirens sit. Odysseus makes all his sailors block their ears with wax and then bind him so that he cannot move and thus he becomes the only man to have heard the Sirens' song and live. Bloom's counterpart to Odysseus' wax is the activity of writing that allows him to escape the sentimental masculinity offered by the singers in the Ormond Bar. Significantly he leaves the bar as Ben Dollard, whose outsize genitals are a thread of both chapter and book, begins to sing 'The Croppy Boy'.

One of the most famous of Irish rebel songs, 'The Croppy Boy' tells the story of`an Irish volunteer of the 1798 rebellion who goes to confession before setting out to battle to confess, among other sins, that he has forgotten to pray for his mother's rest. As he concludes his confession by stating his determination to join the rebels in battle, the priest throws off his cassock to reveal that he is a British soldier who immediately orders the Croppy's execution. The song for Joyce speaks directly to the personal and political anguish in which Stephen finds himself. Stephen is unable to forget his dead mother and is convinced of the joint tyranny of priest and king. The song does not represent the perfidy of the English or the filial piety of the Croppy but the sentimental paralysis of the singers in the bar. The opposition between the playful liberation of writing and the mawkish repression of nationalism ends the chapter.

Bloom has escaped the Sirens but he is aware that he has to fart and stops to look in a shop window which displays a picture of Robert Emmett, another rebel of 1798, whose famous last words Bloom reads: 'When my country takes its place amongst the nations of the earth. Then and not till then let my epitaph be written. I have done' (376). Emmett would delay writing until after national liberation; for Joyce to write now is essential to bring about a liberation which is not repression. *Done* in Emmett's speech from the bar has a singular meaning; Joyce multiplies it by three. It repeats the penultimate phrase of the two pages that have opened the chapter and indicates that the chapter has finished. It provides the final word of Emmett's famous speech and indicates that Bloom has farted:'Pprrpffrrppffff' (376).

Dublin is a city of pubs and we have already visited both Davy Byrne's and the Ormond Bar in the company of Bloom and heard word of Stephen's visit to two Mooney's pubs. Bloom now makes for Barney Kiernan's, where he has promised to discuss Paddy Dignam's affairs with Martin Cunningham. Barney Kiernan's Homeric double is the cave which houses the savage one-eyed giant Polyphemus, who imprisons and eats Odysseus' sailors at a rate of two a day. It is a classic example of Odysseus' unusual range as an epic hero not only that he manages to blind the Cyclops but also that he has earlier and cunningly told Polyphemus that his name is **no one**. When the blinded giant attempts to summon other giants to his aid by roaring that he is being attacked by **no one**, the other giants ignore him.

Joyce's Cyclops chapter is full of nicknames and initials and is in large part recounted by an anonymous narrator whose energetic use of the Dublin demotic is matched only by the fact that he has a bad word to say about everybody. The Nameless One has his account of the events interrupted by alternative descriptions that use completely different discourses to produce very different images of what is taking place in the pub. These interruptions are often generically described as mock heroic but although they begin in what might be called the style of a cod Renaissance epic, they vary from the spiritualist to the scientific, from the parliamentary to the biblical, in a hilarious riot of writing. The multiple identities offered by these parodies, which number more than thirty, contrast with the paralysed fixity of the identifications offered by the central figure of the chapter, who is referred to only as 'the Citizen'.

The Citizen, who has only one eye and is thus both an analogue for the Cyclops and a huge phallic pun, is based on one of the most important cultural figures of the Gaelic revival, Michael Cusack, and Joyce uses this chapter to show his distance from the nationalist rhetoric which was to underpin the Easter Rising of 1916 and the Irish war of independence which ran in tandem with the writing of *Ulysses*. Joyce's argument with the nationalists was not in their political aims. In a lecture that he gave in Trieste in April 1907 he anticipated the emergence of a 'bilingual, republican, self centred and enterprising island' and the Citizen's history of the English exploitation of Ireland is all but copied from this and other lectures and articles that Joyce wrote in Trieste (*Crit.*, 125). Before he left Dublin Joyce began lessons in Irish with Patrick Pearse, who was to become the leader of the Easter Rising, but he abandoned them because he could not stomach Pearse's continual denigration of the English language. Nationalism is toxic for Joyce because it reduces everything to one opposition between the pure Gael and the filthy modern Saxon. Everything the Citizen says is placed in this binary opposition. Just as Emmett would delay writing until national liberation, the Citizen ignores the playful identities offered by the many parodies in favour of a single paralysed identity. When that identity is challenged by Bloom, who is both a Jew and an Irishman, the Citizen reacts with violence. The sentimental nationalism of the Ormond Bar turns toxic and aggressive, but Bloom, aided by Martin Cunningham, makes a heroic exit from the giant's cave.

Ulysses claims to be encyclopedic in its representation of a day in Dublin but it is a radically incomplete encyclopedia. Between Bloom's exit from Barney Kiernan's and his appearance on Sandymount Strand more than two hours have elapsed. While we may surmise that he has been counselling Dignam's widow with Martin Cunningham, we learn nothing of those conversations. Indeed, we do not at first realize that Bloom is part of the scene we are observing. That scene is sketched for us by a young woman called Gerty McDowell, whose head is full of women's magazines and romance novels. The sickly sentiments and stilted syntax of Gerty's thoughts are both repellent and hilarious but the further we read the more we realize that bubbling below this sickly confection is a demotic Dublin speech with which she disparages her friends and a very active libido which focuses on a man sitting on some nearby rocks with whom she indulges in an ever more frank exchange of glances. The action on the beach has two counterpoints—a benediction in a nearby church and a fireworks display. The fireworks offer Gerty an excuse to lean back and expose her knickers to her anonymous admirer and they engage in a prolonged silent sexual encounter. This episode parallels the moment in the *Odyssey* when our epic hero emerges from the sea to find the Princess Nausicaa playing with her handmaidens. It is noteworthy that Joyce's sustained attack on heroism extends to this sexual encounter which has no suggestion of genital penetration.

'Cemetery put in of course on account of the symmetry' (*U*, 154). If you have death you must have birth and the long chapter devoted to birth is The Oxen of the Sun. In Homer the episode focuses on Odysseus' crew committing sacrilege by slaughtering cattle sacred to the Sun God. In Joyce the focus is on the three-day labour of Mina Purefoy and a drunken student party taking place in the same hospital. Joyce was obsessed by the physiological body and particularly fascinated by the development of the embryo, which provides some of the structure of the chapter. Indeed, one could complain that the whole chapter has too much structure.

Most important is the history of the literary language. The chapter progresses from Anglo-Saxon to modern slang as we participate in the drunken conversation of Stephen and his friends. The idea of using different historical stages of the language is a strong one and there are a few good jokes—a tin of sardines described in pre-industrial English; Stephen and Bloom becoming Boasthard and Cautious Calmer in a Bunyan skit—but most of the chapter is very heavy weather. The discussions of Catholic theology of parturition and sexuality in all their misogynistic detail and the dense reflection on creativity which places enormous emphasis on the post-creation (the meaning of the work as an afterthought) are difficult to grasp. There are moments which promise much—the history of protestantism as combining too much grammar with an inordinate emphasis on both the phallus and the individual self—but which dissolve before the promise is redeemed. It must be said that all these faults are features of drunken conversation, which is what Joyce is recording. Finally, the long-delayed birth occurs.

Bloom, ever solicitous of others, had come to enquire after the suffering Mrs Purefoy. He has got caught up in a drunken student party but he is careful not to drink and he becomes worried about his friend Simon's son. Stephen Dedalus has now been drinking since lunch. He has not eaten and is so drunk that he is on the verge of psychosis—the disintegration of the self in extreme drunkenness. Bloom notices first that Stephen is dangerously drunk and then that Mulligan, who comes late to the party, is ready to lead him into harm's way. Bloom's growing concern for Stephen is the narrative pivot of the book because now, unlike in the newspaper office and the library, Bloom and Stephen are in direct relationship. The text does not dwell on this but Bloom is sufficiently worried that he decides to keep Stephen in view as the party adjourns to yet another pub. The text now becomes a jumble of contemporary slang, and both the literary language and the chapter grind to their end.

There is another Joycean cut and we find Leopold Bloom entering Nighttown, Joyce's fictional name for the red light district in Dublin. The text now takes the form of an expressionist drama in which hallucination dominates as Bloom continues to pursue Stephen, whom he has lost in Westland Row train station. These hallucinations include long political sequences in which Bloom becomes Lord Mayor of Dublin and an equally long trial at which society women of Dublin accuse Bloom of shameful sexual harassment. At the same time characters from earlier in the book reassemble in new guises and settings. A full analysis of Circe, which is also the longest chapter of *Ulysses*, would be a full analysis of the novel itself. However, one can point to two narrative climaxes in the brothel where Bloom finally finds Stephen—Bloom's transformation into a woman and Stephen's breaking of the brothel lamp.

Freud and Joyce shared a belief in bisexuality as fundamental to the human condition and Freud's powerful argument on fetishism makes an interesting footnote to one thread of both novel and chapter. Bloom's fetish, the potato which he carries everywhere, is signalled early in the novel but it only becomes a feature of the text when Bloom encounters his mother Ellen Higgins in the phantasmographic world of Nighttown. She lifts her skirts and out tumbles a 'shrivelled potato' (570). For Freud fetishism is a psychic mechanism which the little boy adopts when he is faced with the appalling fact that the mother has no penis. The small boy creates a substitute for the missing penis, which threatens his being with annihilation—he could have been different. This substitute allows him to disavow the fact of sexual difference. He both believes the evidence of sexual difference and yet has a talisman which allows him to disavow with security this annihilating thought. When Bloom enters into the final stages of his Walpurgisnacht he gives up this security.

Zoe, the only one of the prostitutes in Bella Cohen's brothel who radiates sexuality, begins to flirt with him and explore his clothes. When she gets to his trouser pocket she is shocked to find a hard object which she takes to be a syphilitic chancre. In the face of Bloom's denial, she takes action:

> (*Her hand slides into his left trouser pocket and brings out a hard black shrivelled potato. She regards it and Bloom with dumb moist lips.*)
>
> BLOOM: A talisman. Heirloom.
>
> ZOE: For Zoe? For keeps? For being so nice, eh?
>
> (*She puts the potato greedily into a pocket, then links his arm, cuddling him with supple warmth. He smiles uneasily.*) (599–600)

Bloom has every reason to be uneasy; he has lost his magic protection against thinking of the reality of sexual difference and fifty pages later he becomes a woman. The exit from fantasy is signalled by the return of the potato:

> BLOOM (*gently*) Give me back that potato, will you?
>
> ZOE: Forfeits, a fine thing and a superfine thing.
>
> BLOOM (*with feeling*) It is nothing, but still a relic of poor mama. (663)

I am not suggesting that there is any direct influence of Freud on Circe in particular or *Ulysses* in general. Apart from anything else, Freud's essay on fetishism was published in 1927, five years after *Ulysses*. Indeed, Joyce is relentlessly opposed to psychoanalysts, damning them in *Finnegans Wake* as those who prey upon the 'yung and easily freudened' (*FW* 22–3).

Despite joint concerns with sex and language, Joyce found Freud's rigid interpretations anathema. But there can be no doubting that the family of *Finnegans Wake* swapping and multiplying sexual identities is Freud's child endlessly questioning his or her engenderment in the bodies and desires of the parents. There are many parallels but some differences. For Freud teaches that the Oedipal relationship between father and son is one of rivalry. The son is only able to join adult human society at the point at which he accepts the father's dominance, in particular that he must renounce all thoughts of the mother's body.

Jacques Lacan, the French psychoanalyst who has some claim to be the most important of Freud's successors, objected to this account, arguing that it made the renunciation both too conscious and not necessary enough. Lacan distinguished between the intersubjective world of the imagination in which the father and son were engaged in a conscious rivalry for absolute power and the social world of the symbolic which revealed this absolute power as a fantasy. The entry into the world of the social is the moment at which the child internalizes the knowledge that the father is not an all-powerful sexual being but is himself articulated in the social world of desire. The imaginary castration that the child fears will be visited on its body is replaced by the symbolic castration that the father has himself suffered as the price of his access to the social.

Stephen's problem at the beginning of the book is that he longs for an all-powerful father that he can become. This poisonous fantasy, all the more venomous in Ireland where fathers were castrated in their own imagination by English imperialism, is dissolved in Epps's cocoa at 7 Eccles Street where a Triestino father offers a different model of development. Stephen is prepared for this lesson by the moment in Circe when on the verge of psychotic collapse he accidentally breaks a lamp in Bella Cohen's brothel. It is the intervention of chance that saves him; the recognition of chance is the final repudiation of the all-powerful child that his mother so desires. It is also for Joyce the recognition of the Irish son that he cannot have. Bloom's hallucinated vision of his dead son Rudy, which ends Circe, clothes him in a motley of garments which mix the dress of the English middle classes and the Gaelic revival. There could be no clearer sign of how such a child was an impossibility for Joyce.

The end of Circe is the end of Joyce's Odyssey. In Homer's tale the return to Ithaca and the meeting with the old shepherd Eumaeus comes long before the end of the story but Joyce now has only three of his eighteen chapters remaining. The text signals that this is the third and final section, traditionally referred to as the Nostos (homecoming). The first chapter, Eumaeus, is a delight. All day Bloom has been dwelling on 'Matcham's masterstroke', the story that he had read at stool in the morning and which has given him the idea of penning a story drawn from life that will augment his income: 'To improve the shining hour he wondered whether he might meet with anything approaching the same luck as Mr Philip

Beaufoy if taken down in writing. Suppose he were to pen
something out of the common groove (as he fully intended doing)
at the rate of one guinea per column, *My Experiences*, let us say, *in
a Cabman's Shelter*' (750). Bloom's problem is that, although there
may be a touch of the artist about old Bloom, he is, unlike his
major model Schmitz, who published novels under the pen name
Italo Svevo, no writer. He is also exhausted after a day full of
incident.

The result is that the prose of his *Experiences in a Cabman's
Shelter* is woeful. Clauses dangle from each other, as sentences fail
to come to an end, repeat, double back, and do everything except
flow. Nowhere is Joyce's genius as a writer more evident than in
this chapter as he authors a terribly carpentered prose which both
engages and provokes constant laughter. He also mines his source
text one more time to come up with a version of Odysseus that he
has neglected up till now. Homer's hero is a pathological liar who
is no sooner introduced to a stranger than he invents a new past
and name for himself. This reaches a vertiginous climax in
Homer's epic when Odysseus returns to Ithaca and lies about his
identity to his old servant Eumaeus, his son Telemachus, his wife
Penelope, and his father Laertes amongst others. He is a fertile
liar in that each false past and identity is new. There has been
none of this Odysseus in Bloom, but he appears in the sailor in the
cabman's shelter who claims with little evidence to be called
D. B. Murphy and to have sailed all the seven seas. Murphy can't
move his lips without lying but he dominates the conversation in
the cabman's shelter.

Truth to tell, the reader who is expecting a crucial recognition
scene between Bloom and Stephen will be disappointed. Stephen
is still drunk and cantankerous, Bloom caught up in his
meandering prose. In any case Joyce has already made clear his
contempt for narrative closures which guarantee secure identities.
The final sentence of the chapter mocks the reader who has been
waiting for such a moment as the duo walk out of earshot: '...they

at times stopped and walked again, continuing their *tête à tête*...about sirens, enemies of man's reason, mingled with a number of other topics of the same category, usurpers, historical cases of the kind...' (775–6).

Ithaca, the penultimate chapter of the novel, is a little more promising. Joyce has continuously kept the emotional temperature low in *Ulysses* but Ithaca is the fridge of the book. The catechistic style privileges information over emotion and the form gives as much weight to the Roundwood reservoir in Wicklow when Bloom turns on the tap as to Bloom and Stephen's discovery that they both knew Dante Riordan, so memorable a figure in the first chapter of *A Portrait*. However Bloom and Stephen are now talking and if the style refuses to differentiate between fact and emotion, a sense of fellowship, slight in the cabman's shelter, is now palpable. Indeed everything is preparing us for the narrative climax of the book when we are shocked by an episode so inexplicable that almost no Joyce critic has dared to comment on it and the few that do comment tend to dismiss it as inexplicable.

Joyce and Bloom have been talking of Gaelic and Hebrew and this leads to Bloom singing the Zionist anthem in Hebrew. He only sings the first two lines because they are all he can remember (just as Stephen doesn't know Gaelic, Bloom doesn't know Hebrew) but he paraphrases the rest. Stephen now stands up to sing. In life Joyce was devoted to song and singing but in *Ulysses* music is a siren song which lures hearer and singer into false fellowship. The parallels between Hebrew and Gaelic which Stephen and Bloom have been discussing would suggest that Stephen should now sing a Gaelic patriotic song. There is no question of such a song because Stephen doesn't speak Gaelic. There is also no question of the sentimental songs of Irish nationalism like 'The Croppy Boy' which have received a final *coup de grâce* in the maelstrom of Circe. What Stephen does sing, however, is an anti-Semitic song. At the moment of recognition, of the narrative climax of the whole novel, Stephen sings to Bloom not simply an anti-Semitic song but a song deeply rooted in English anti-Semitism.

The blood libel, that Jews kill Christian children for their blood, is one of the oldest and most persistent of European anti-Semitic tropes. In England its dominant version stretches back to events in Lincoln in the mid-thirteeenth century when it was claimed that a little boy named Hugh was ritually sacrificed by Jews. There are many versions of this history and Joyce's song is one of them. It is given extra weight in the text by the fact that it is not one of the numerous extant versions (including songs from which the anti-Semitic elements have been purged) but is Joyce's own version with the words written out in his handwriting and the music also supplied.

The song tells of a little boy ('Harry Hughes') who twice kicks a ball through the window of a Jew's house and on the second occasion is lured inside by the Jew's daughter, who cuts off his 'little head'. Stephen's very dense commentary turns the boy into a predestined victim who goes to his death 'consenting' (810). The psychoanalytic account of a symbolic castration as a necessary cost of access to the social order finds expression in the ritual of circumcision. It might be tempting to read Stephen's song and commentary as talking of circumcision ('little head') rather than murder. The problem with such a reading is that it rests very heavily on the word 'consenting'. It also ignores the fact that Bloom is not in any way comforted by Stephen's commentary. He may not know Stephen's song but he recognizes Jew hatred when he hears it, particularly as the Jew's daughter in the song makes him think of his own daughter Milly, who has been in and out of his thoughts all day.

This rather elaborate interpretation has some merit but a simpler reading is to be found in the importance of Hugh of Lincoln for the history of English literature. Chaucer's The Prioress's Tale, which is another version of the blood libel, ends with a reference to Hugh of Lincoln. Shakespeare has already been judged no model for a writer because of his sexual possessiveness; this song might remind us that Chaucer is as badly tainted with anti-Semitism. English literature is no model for an Irish writer.

But then neither is Ireland. When Deasy makes his anti-Semitic joke that the Irish never persecuted the Jews because they never let them in he lies twice. It is true that very few Jews chose impoverished Ireland as a future home. But some did; Limerick for example had a population of about 130 Jews at the turn of the century. It was in Limerick in January of 1904 that a Redemptorist priest delivered a savagely anti-Semitic speech calling for a boycott that would drive the Jewish community out of Limerick. The resulting conflict—both police and protestants backed the Jews—lasted some two years and drove five Jewish families out of Limerick. The boycott was much reported and discussed in Ireland and is undoubtedly one of the elements that feeds into the Jewish elements in *Ulysses*. It may be that Stephen in singing this song is matching Bloom's Zionist anthem with his own Irish anti-Semitic anthem.

While Bloom is upset by the song and it opens up onto thoughts of ritual murder, he calms himself by thinking back on episodes in Milly's life and he ends this train of thought by asking Stephen if he will stay for the night, an offer which Stephen amiably and gratefully declines.

The final chapter of *Ulysses* brings a new voice to the novel as Molly Bloom lies in bed reflecting on her day and her life. Molly's monologue was greeted early as a historic breakthrough of a woman's voice articulating sexual desire in unprecedented ways. Later, feminists pointed out that Molly was actually written by a man and that the identification of woman with sexuality is one of the longest-lived of male fantasies. Maud Ellmann in a typically brilliant essay, '"Penelope" without the Body', argues convincingly that both positions ignore the fact that Penelope is above all a written text and that what is written avoids many of these easy equations.

Penelope started life as letters. There is no doubt that something of the style and idiom of Molly's letters are borrowed from the letters of Nora Barnacle. Indeed Joyce first conceived this chapter as a series of letters. But then he abandoned the epistolary form for a 'feminine monologue', which is how the technique of the chapter is described in one of the elaborate schemas that Joyce drew up to gloss his book. The first reading of this feminine monologue is a dizzying experience as the eight 2,500-word sentences have no punctuation and Molly often uses the pronoun 'he' to pivot from one masculine subject to another. Interestingly, however, on closer reading Molly's stream of consciousness is more syntactically regular than Bloom's or Stephen's. It is true that Molly is relatively indifferent to the difference between the men that drift in and out of her thoughts and that she often shifts topic without signal, but that gives more weight to the last prolonged memory of the kiss on the hill of Howth where 'he' is most definitely Leopold Bloom.

Penelope leaves Homer behind. There is no equivalent chapter in the *Odyssey*. Indeed the literary model here is Joyce's favourite poet, Dante. Dante not only used the medieval Latin Ulysses as his name for the Greek hero (and not Virgil's classical Ulix), but he also has Ulysses, bored and idle in Ithaca, setting out on the ultimate adventure—to sail through the Pillars of Hercules, beyond the boundaries of the known world. The Pillars of Hercules was the classical world's name for the Straits of Gibraltar and Joyce's desire for *Ulysses* to emulate Dante as well as Homer is certainly one of the reasons that Molly is born in Gibraltar and that many of her memories are of her girlhood in southern Spain. As, if not more, important is Gibraltar's contemporary status as key, both symbolically and militarily, to the British Empire, a protestant redoubt in southern Europe and, after the opening of the Suez Canal, the gateway to India and the East. Many of Molly's memories are composed of love and kisses, and although Gibraltar as a military garrison is there as a backdrop one can read much of the chapter, often explicitly, as an Irish girl's resistance to British military rule.

Molly remembers Gibraltar but she also remembers Dublin and many of her memories provide a cutting view of the men who have patronized her earlier in the novel. The most critically remarked function of the chapter is to accomplish a Homeric slaughter of the suitors. The *Odyssey* ends in an orgy of blood and death as the suitors are butchered in the palace that they have abused for so long. Joyce long thought that he could find no place for blood or death as he ended his *Ulysses*: Molly menstruating provided one and her symbolic scorn for her suitors the other. All good comedies end with a marriage. We get no memories of the moment at the altar, no flashbacks to the bed of penetrative sex. However we do get the required response at the altar as the climax to the memory of their first lingual kiss on Howth Head. The single word yes repeated so perfectly to end chapter and book celebrates Molly and Poldy's union but in saying yes to that we are saying yes to a dysfunctional marriage. To which Joyce might reply that 'dysfunctional marriage' is a tautology.

However Joyce is requiring us to say yes to much more and much worse than that. From his moment of insane sexual jealousy in 1909, Joyce knew that the task he had set himself was monumental. *A Portrait* provided a way out, but to affirm his being in all its drunken and perverse reality he had to go back in. He could not make all of his being live by cutting himself off from Dublin, he had to become Dublin with all the squalor and pain, all the wit and drunkenness, all the repression visited by the Church and the unspeakable humiliation of being a subject people. Stephen could leave Ireland so blithely at the end of *A Portrait* because he had already returned as Joyce wrote the opening chapters of *Ulysses* alongside the final chapters of *A Portrait*. *Ulysses* was written so that he could live; he wished the whole of his being to speak and his whole being included every aspect of Dublin.

The ethic of *Ulysses* is severe: All or not at all.

Chapter 5
Finnegans Wake

Ulysses was not only finished but published to undreamt of acclaim. Harriet Shaw Weaver had made sure that Joyce had ample funds for the rest of his life. He was living in Paris, which had always been his first choice of exile. His children had moved into a more difficult stage as they transitioned in and out of their third national educational system in yet a third language but they were not yet a sorrow rather than a joy.

It was in these favourable circumstances that Joyce began to write a book which was to take him seventeen years to complete. It was circulated in fragments as *Work in Progress* through two decades but finally was published in 1939 as *Finnegans Wake*. In *Finnegans Wake* Joyce attempted to write a book which would take all history and knowledge for its subject matter and the workings of the dreaming mind for its form. If one takes a page at random from *Finnegans Wake*, one may find reference to subjects as disparate as chemistry, Irish mythology, philosophy, American history, details from Joyce's life, all woven together in a language which constantly creates new words by fusing and shortening old ones or by borrowing from the many European languages that Joyce knew.

The result of this deformation of language is that every word carries more than one meaning and each sentence opens out onto an infinity of interpretations. Joyce rarely defended his work directly after *A Portrait*. But on the few occasions when he did he continued to talk in terms of realism. Joyce's eye was caught in 1929 by an article in *Harper's* by young American leftist Max Eastman decrying the confusion of two tendencies in much modern writing. There was a tendency, which Eastman approved of, to abandon the interpretation of existence. However, Eastman argued that this positive tendency had become confused with a failure to communicate experience intelligibly. Joyce was apparently impressed enough by this argument that he asked Sylvia Beach to arrange a meeting with the young man where Joyce championed his writing by appeal to the reality of the sleeping mind. Eastman published Joyce's thoughts in the October 1931 edition of *Harper's*: 'In writing of the night I really could not, I felt I could not, use words in their ordinary connections. Used that way they do not express how things are in the night, in the different stages—the conscious, then semi-conscious, then unconscious. I found that it could not be done with words in their ordinary relations and connections' (*JJ*, 546).

The difficulty of the language is compounded by difficulty of divining what story this extraordinary language is recounting. Figures change name and transform themselves into their opposites, appear and disappear without any obvious rationality. Joyce's claim for his method was that it enabled the articulation of areas of experience which were barred from conventional language and plot. He told Miss Weaver: 'One great part of every human existence is passed in a state which cannot be rendered sensible by the use of wideawake language, cutanddry grammar and goahead plot' (*JJ*, 597).

Many critics have complained that Joyce's last book marks a major change from his earlier work and that his interest in language had become a self-indulgent aberration. However all Joyce's writing focuses on the methods by which identity is produced in language. In the opening passage of *A Portrait* we move from the paternal narrator who tells us a story and fixes an identity (the listening child realizes that he is baby tuckoo and that he can locate himself in a definite spatio-temporal identity) to the mother's voice in which stories are dissolved into the sounds, smells, and sensations of the body. It is the deformation of language as the child falls asleep 'O, the green wothe botheth' that signals the transition to a world where the material of language (the sound of 'Tralala') has dominance over meaning. The identity of the story gets lost in the confused and disparate experiences of the body.

While the father fixes with his eye, the mother displaces into the world of the ear. On the one hand we find the self and the father, the authority of meaning and society, and, on the other hand, we find the body and the mother, the subversive force of sound and desire. This movement from identity to infancy is one that we repeat each night as we enter the timeless world of dreams where words become things, and we reverse the process each morning as we wake to the temporal continuity of meaning. Language changes its nature in the passage between these two realms. A normal syntax and morphology (cutanddry grammar) is appropriate to the normality of stories (goahead plot) but as soon as we begin to pay attention to the material constituents of words in either the spoken or written form then we find ourselves slipping into the world of desire. And this eruption of the material of language is not confined to the sleeping life or dreams. Jokes and verbal slips are the most obvious example in our waking life when another order of language interrupts the normal flow of communication. When Joyce claimed that in *Finnegans Wake* he was investigating a 'great part of every human existence' which escaped normal linguistic relations, he was not simply claiming to represent accurately a sleeping mind but rather to be investigating a vital dimension of our being which, although more evident in dreams, insists in our waking life as well. His earlier works and their experiments with narrative and language made the writing of *Finnegans Wake* possible but both his methods and his topics remain remarkably constant throughout his adult life.

The importance of the opposition between the invisible language of the story and the material language of desire is evident throughout *Finnegans Wake* but it is towards the end as Anna Livia, both mother and river, flows to her death that it is stated in one of its simplest forms. As Anna thinks back over her past life, she remembers how much her husband (the ubiquitous figure who is indicated by the letters HCE) wanted a daughter, hoping for a female in the family who would believe his stories, who would give to him the respect that he feels is his due. But the father is inevitably disappointed for the mother teaches her daughter that beneath the stories and the identities lies a world of letters and desire. While the father tells the son stories, the mother teaches the daughter the alphabet: 'If you spun your yarns to him on the swishbarque waves I was spelling my yearns to her over cottage cake' (*FW*, 620). The father's yarns (stories) are displaced by the mother's yearns (desires); telling gives way to spelling. It is this struggle between meaning and sound, between story and language, between male and female that *Finnegans Wake* enacts, introducing the reader to a world in which his or her own language can suddenly reveal new desires beneath old meanings as the material of language forms and reforms.

If the language attempts to investigate the processes by which we are constructed in the world of sense and syntax, the stories that we piece together from the mosaic of the *Wake* constantly return us to the place of that construction: the family. As the text throws out references to the world's religions and philosophies, to geography and astronomy, we come back again and again to the most banal and local of all problems. What is the nature of the obscure sexual offence the father, HCE, is charged with? And is he guilty? Only the mother, Anna Livia Plurabelle, ALP, seems to know the definitive answers to these questions. The mother has written or will write (tenses become interchangeable in the timeless world of the *Wake*) a letter which will explain all, but the letter is difficult to identify and decipher. It was dictated to one of her sons, Shem, a writer of ill repute, who is likely to have altered the contents, and may have been delivered by her other son, Shaun, a nauseating worldly success. The two brothers are engaged in constant conflict, often occasioned by sexual rivalry. In some obscure way their sister, Issy, might hold the solution to the problems of her father and brothers but she refuses to say anything at all serious as she is quite content to gaze endlessly at herself in the mirror.

If language, the family, and sexuality provide three of the emphases of Joyce's last work, there is a fourth which is as important: death. Indeed the title of the book, *Finnegans Wake*, makes clear this concern. The immediate reference is to a song of almost identical title (only an apostrophe differentiates them): 'Finnegan's Wake'. This tells the story of an Irish bricklayer who went to work one morning with a terrible hangover and, as a result, fell off his ladder. His friends presume that he is dead and take him home to 'wake' him, that is to spend the night before the funeral drinking beside the dead body. During the wake a fight breaks out and a bottle of whiskey breaks by Tim's head. No sooner has some whiskey trickled into his mouth than he revives and joins in the fun of his own funeral (which thus becomes a '*funferal*' (*FW*, 120). The ambiguity of the 'wake' of Joyce's title, which refers both to part of the funeral process (Finnegan's wake) and to the general awakening of all the Finnegans (*Finnegans Wake* without an apostrophe), indicates the inseparability of life and death in the world of language. To come to life, to recognize one's own separate existence, is also to allow the possibility of its termination, its end. *Finnegans Wake* not only puns on two meanings of 'wake' but the first word contains both an end ('fin' is French for 'end') and a new beginning ('egan' tells us that everything will start 'again'). And this process will be the negation (negans) of the ordinary processes of language, an attention to the trace ('wake' in its third sense) left by the passage of language. The clarity of communication will be disturbed by the material trace of the letter that any communication leaves in its wake.

Death and sexuality, the construction of language within the family drama—Joyce's text is no self-indulgent whim but an engagement with the very matter of our being. In his attempt to break away from the 'evidences' of conventional narrative with its fixed causality and temporality, two Italian thinkers, Giordano Bruno and Giambattista Vico, were of profound importance in the writing of *Finnegans Wake*. In understanding the importance of these figures it is not enough to sketch the positive features of their thought, one must also understand what Joyce is avoiding by his use of these theorists, what presuppositions he is denying.

Giordano Bruno was a philosopher of the Italian Renaissance. After becoming a Dominican friar he flirted with the varieties of Protestant reformism as well as interesting himself in hermetic philosophy. His unorthodox beliefs and his final death at the stake as a heretic in 1600 had fascinated Joyce from an early age. Bruno's principle of the 'coincidence of contraries' denied the existence of absolute identities in the universe. Bruno argued that oppositions collapsed into unities at their extremes, thus extreme heat and extreme cold were held to be indistinguishable, and all identities were, therefore, provisional. Bruno joined this belief to a belief in an infinite universe composed of an infinity of worlds.

There is an obvious level at which such theories offer some explanations of both the constant transformation of characters into their opposites in *Finnegans Wake* and the infinite worlds opened up by the 'dream within a dream' structure of the text. But to understand Joyce as simply providing an artistic gloss to the theories of an obscure philosopher is to minimize the importance of the *Wake*. Bruno is important insofar as he provides a theoretical trellis on which the philosophical and linguistic presuppositions of identity can be unpicked. At one level of consciousness we claim an identity and stability both for ourselves and our objects of perception. But such identities can only be produced by a process of differentiation in which other identities are rejected. This rejection, however, presupposes that other identities exist. The paradoxical feature of identity is that its conditions of existence allow the possibility of its very contradiction. It is the play of identity that Joyce investigates in the *Wake* where language no longer has to presuppose non-contradiction and everybody becomes everybody else in an infinite series of substitutions and juxtapositions which never attain some imaginary finality but constantly break, re-form, and start again.

Giambattista Vico is, arguably, even more important to the structure and content of *Finnegans Wake*. His name occurs (in suitably distorted form) in the opening sentence of the book as does a reference to his cyclical theory of history. A Neapolitan philosopher of the 18th century, Vico was one of the first to propose a general theory of historical change. He held that history was a cyclical process in which civilization proceeded from a theocratic to an aristocratic to a democratic age and that, at the end of the democratic age, civilization passed through a short period of destruction, the *ricorso*, which recommenced the cycle.

The very plan of *Finnegans Wake*, with its three long books and a short concluding one, bears witness to Vico's importance. It is not only Vico's historical theories which figure in the Wake, there is also much play with his account of the birth of language and civilization. According to Vico, primitive man, surprised in the sexual act by a clap of thunder, is stricken with fear and guilt at what he imagines is the angered voice of God. He retires into a cave to conceal his activities and it is this act which inaugurates civilization. Language arises when man attempts to reproduce the sound of thunder with his own vocal organs. Once again, however, it would be wrong to understand Joyce's use of Vico as the artistic illustration of philosophical theses. What Vico's theory offers is both an initial articulation of language, sexuality, and society and, more importantly, a theory to oppose to dominant historicist accounts of history and an account of language which does not privilege any particular people. Historicism understands the historical process to be subordinate to a dominant principle, which can only be understood in terms of the 'end' to which it is progressing.

When Stephen Dedalus and Mr Deasy discuss history in the second chapter of *Ulysses*, Mr Deasy claims that 'All history moves toward one great goal, the manifestation of God' (*U*, 42). This historicism imposes on the individual a meaning in which he is already defined. Stephen refuses such a meaning and identity when he claims that God is simply a noise in the street, the undifferentiated sound from which we fabricate meaning. It is by plunging into this sound that we can unmake the meanings imposed on us and awake from the nightmare of history into the dream of language. By insisting on the infinite repeatability of any moment, by refusing a progression to history, one can refuse the ready-made identities offered to us in order to investigate the reality of the processes that construct us. By denying an end to history, we can participate in the infinite varieties of the present. Bruno and Vico are used in *Finnegans Wake* to aid the deconstruction of identity into difference and to replace progress with repetition. But if Joyce used these thinkers it was largely to displace the dominant conceptions of the everyday novel of identity and temporality and not because they hold some intrinsic truth.

To attempt a summary of the events of *Finnegans Wake* is both necessary and misleading. Necessary in that there are strands of narrative that we can follow through the text, misleading in that such narratives are always dispersed into other narratives. In a book of this length it is only possible to look at one of the seventeen chapters of the *Wake*, and I have chosen chapter 7 of Book 1, the portrait of Shem the Penman, as one of the more immediately accessible sections of the text.

The six chapters that lead up to it have taken us through both a synopsis of all the themes of the book (chapter 1) and then through a series of accounts of HCE's obscure and unmentionable crime and his trial (chapters 2–4). The letter which is so crucial to an understanding of all the issues at stake is discussed in chapter 5. Chapter 6 is composed of a set of questions and answers about the characters discussed in the letter and ends with a question about Shem. The whole of chapter 7 (the one we shall consider in a little more detail) is devoted to Shem the writer and at the end of this chapter he gives way to his mother, Anna Livia, whose life and activities are discussed in chapter 8.

Book 2 transfers the scene from the whole city of Dublin to a particular public house in Chapelizod, one of Dublin's suburbs. In chapter 1 the children play outside the pub; in chapter 2 they have been put to bed in one of the rooms above the bar where they conduct their night lessons, lessons which intermingle academic subjects with the discovery of sexuality. Chapter 3 takes place in the bar over which the children are sleeping. Customers and publican (HCE) gossip the evening away and when they have all left the innkeeper falls asleep on the floor in a drunken stupor and dreams about the story of Tristram and Iseult, this dream composing the major topic of chapter 4.

Book 3 finds the innkeeper asleep in bed and chapters 1–3 deal with Shaun in his various manifestations as man of the world. At the end of chapter 3 Shaun dissolves into the voice of other characters and in chapter 4 the father and mother, woken by the cries of one of the children, make rather unsatisfactory love as dawn breaks.

Book 4 sees the coming of dawn and the start of a new cycle. The mother Anna Livia is now old and looks back over her past life before she dissolves into the sea of death which starts the cycle again. The final unfinished sentence of the book ends with the word 'the'. Joyce chose the definite article as the most common and least significant word in the English language. It also had the advantage of being both the last and the first word of the book, for the book is an unending cycle and the last sentence is finished by the first sentence of the book.

The portrait of Shem (*FW*, 169–95) is unflattering in the extreme. He is accused of endless crimes and perversions. The officious tone of the opening sentences suggests that it is the rival brother, Shaun, speaking. Shaun, a pillar of society and an exemplar of moral rectitude, accuses Shem of refusing to be a proper member of society. To this end Shaun employs every kind of racist and anti-Semitic slur. Shem is accused of being a sham and a forger, never able to be himself, to assume a definite identity, but constantly imitating others in his writing. His immense pride goes together with an absolute refusal to join in the patriotic struggle which would offer him the chance of achieving true manhood. Instead he prefers to occupy himself with the affairs of women. Shaun describes the particularly obscene process by which Shem's books are composed (we will look in detail at this description) and how Shem was arrested because of his books.

After we have read the details of the arrest, we find ourselves at a trial where Shaun, in the person of Justius, tries Shem, in the person of Mercius. Mercius is accused of irreligion, of corrupting women, of squandering money, and, most importantly, of being mad. It would seem that Mercius (Shem) is going to be unable to answer the last charge (the quintessential accusation aimed at those who refuse to conform), but, at the last moment, Anna Livia speaks through his mouth and evades Justius' (Shaun's) accusations. The process by which the mother speaks through the son reduplicates the whole effort of writing *Finnegans Wake*, in which the mother is finally given a voice. Shaun's demand that Shem identify himself, the policeman's request for identification, is avoided by a throwing into doubt of sexual identity. The apparatus by which the police of identity control the progress of history can be undercut by the assertion of an interminable, never complete, bisexuality.

If this imperfect summary indicates some of the drift of the chapter on Shem, we can now look, in a little more detail, at the description of Shem's method of writing. The lines in question

occur after an explanation, in Latin, of the alchemical operations
by which the body's waste matter is transformed into ink with the
aid of a perverted religious prayer:

> Then, pious Eneas, conformant to the fulminant firman which
> enjoins on the tremylose terrian that, when the call comes, he shall
> produce nichthemerically from his unheavenly body a no uncertain
> quantity of obscene matter not protected by copriright in the
> United Stars of Ourania or bedeed and bedood and bedang and
> bedung to him, with this double dye, brought to blood heat, gallic
> acid on iron ore, through the bowels of his misery, flashly, faithly,
> nastily, appropriately, this Esuan Menschavik and the first till last
> alshemist wrote over every square inch of the only foolscap
> available, his own body, till by its corrosive sublimation one
> continuous present tense integument slowly unfolded all
> marryvoising moodmoulded cyclewheeling history (thereby, he
> said, reflecting from his own individual person life unlivable,
> transaccidentated through the slow fires of consciousness into a
> dividual chaos, perilous, potent, common to allflesh, human only,
> mortal) but with each word that would not pass away the squidself
> which he had squirtscreened from the crystalline world wanted
> chagreenold and doriangrayer in its dudhud.   (FW, 185–6)

We can get an initial perspective on how this sentence functions
by examining earlier versions which occur in Joyce's notebooks.
The first, very short, draft of chapter 7 contains some preliminary
suggestions, in Latin, of the equation between writing and
excretion which the final text insists on but there is no hint of the
English passage we are considering. In the next draft, however, we
can read: '**With the dye he wrote minutely, appropriately over
every part of the only foolscap available, his own body, till
integument slowly unfolded universal history & that self which
he hid from the world grew darker & darker in outlook**.' Joyce
then started to revise the sentence (all additions are **in bold**):
'With the **double** dye he wrote minutely, appropriately over every
part of the only foolscap available, his own body, till **one**

integument slowly unfolded universal history **the reflection from his individual person of life unlivable transaccidentated in the slow fire of consciousness into a dividual chaos, perilous, potent, common to all flesh, mortal only, &** that self which he hid from the world grew darker & darker in its outlook.'

In the first version of the sentence we are given an account of how the writer produces his work. The sentence is not syntactically difficult or lexically complex with the exception of the word 'integument' which means a 'covering' or 'skin' and which refers here to the parchment, the material on which the text is written. The text itself is, of course, *Finnegans Wake* (a universal and atemporal history) but it is also earlier manuscripts. There is no question of understanding writing as an aesthetic production of a disembodied and creative mind; to write is to engage in a transaction between body and language, word and flesh. It is not surprising that this activity may seem to resemble the small infant's play with all the parts and productions of his body for throughout *Finnegans Wake* adult behaviour is never far distant from children's play and fantasy. But if the writer is transforming his body into the text we are reading, his self, hidden from the world, is becoming more and more pessimistic.

The first additions emphasize that Joyce is working with a 'double dye' (both ink and excrement) which he is transforming into the 'one integument' that we are reading. The major addition to the text ('the reflections' to 'mortal only') is one of the clearest statements of the process that produces *Finnegans Wake*. The text starts from the 'unlivable' life of the 'individual' and 'transaccidentates' it into a 'dividual chaos'. The invented word 'transaccidentated' refers to the Catholic Mass and to the doctrine of transubstantiation, which holds that the consecrated bread has been transformed into the body of Christ. The Church explains this process with reference to the Aristotelian distinction between the essential nature of a thing (its substance) and the inessential features (its accidents). After the consecration in the Mass, the bread is merely an 'accident' while the 'substance' is Christ's body. Joyce's writing also involves a transformation of the body but there is no question of an appeal to any ultimate 'substance'. Shem's whole life is a series of accidents, both in the modern sense of 'unfortunate and arbitrary events' and in the philosophical sense that Shem is all inessential features ('accidents') without any essential identity ('substance'). Through concentrating on the 'accidental', the writing unmakes the 'individual' to investigate the 'dividual chaos' that constitutes the 'unlivable life'. The presuppositions of identity are displaced to reveal the divisions from which we are all fabricated into unity.

In the text's final version we find that Joyce has added a proper name ('**Eneas**'), a demonstrative phrase ('**this Esuan Menschavik**') and a definite description ('**the first till last alshemist**') to expand the pronoun 'he' at the beginning of the sentence. The first proper name is modified by a clause governed by a present participle modelled on the Latin ('**conformant…**'). This clause in turn contains a relative clause ('**which enjoins…**') which contains within it a further subordinate clause ('**that…he shall…or bedeed…**') which is itself modified by an adverbial clause of time ('**when the call comes**'). The effect of this syntactic complexity is that one has a tendency to read each clause or phrase in a variety of relations with surrounding groups of words. Without seriously transgressing the rules of English syntax at any stage, Joyce so confuses the reader that although each grammatical step will be followed, the phrases and words begin to function outside any grammatical relationship, taking on a multitude of meanings.

At the same time Joyce repeats, with variations, the main theme of the sentence as well as introducing topics from elsewhere in the book. Vico's thunder God makes an appearance in '**fulminant firman**' (through the Latin *fulmen*, a thunderbolt). The equation between excretion and writing is emphasized by the pun 'when the call comes', which is both the call of nature and the writer's vocation. A further term is added to this equation with the introduction of a set of chemical references which link writing to digestion. The first meaning one might attach to '**tremylose**' would be *tremulous*, fearful, but the -ose suffix is a biochemical suffix, indicating a sugar. Similarly '**nichthemerically**' suggests some bio-chemical process although the 'nicht' refers to the nocturnal (night) and the negative (through the German *nicht*, not) features of the writing of *Finnegans Wake*.

The references to copyright and the United States of America are to Joyce's own lawsuits in that country where *Ulysses* was both condemned as obscene and published without Joyce's permission. It thus provides more details of Shem's life but the presence of 'anus' in '**Ourania**' and 'copro' (Greek for dung) in '**copriright**' insist on the presence of the body in all Shem's activities.

The opening phrase of the final version ('**Then, pious Eneas**') illustrates a common device of the *Wake* in quoting famous phrases from European literature in a context which robs them of their sense. The phrase is used frequently in Virgil's epic *The Aeneid*, where it functions in the narrative as an indication that one part of the action is finished and another is about to begin. Within the *Wake* such a phrase merely emphasizes that we are reading a narrative which has no ability to distinguish between ends and beginnings as everything is written in an atemporal present. The other description conferred on Shem ('this Esuan Menschavik') confirms the charge that Shem is a loser in the game of life as it identifies him with Esau (who lost his birthright to Isaac) and the Mensheviks (who lost to the Bolsheviks in the Russian Revolution).

If we now turn to the end of the sentence and look at the transformation from the first draft to the final version then we find once again that the simple meaning has been multiplied through a series of lexical coinages and literary references. The original version claims that there is a correspondence between the degeneration of the artist's self and the production of the book from the material of his body. The final version states that the worlds that he is producing will not disappear and that the self which he had tried to hide behind the skirts of women and squirts of ink ('**squirtscreened**') is becoming sadder and older as it is affected by the book. Joyce also adds a coinage '**doriangrayer**', that refers to Oscar Wilde's *The Picture of Dorian Gray*, a story of a beautiful young man whose picture ages although he, himself, remains young. In its confusion of art and life, of body and representation, Wilde's story is also Joyce's. But the particular confusion of art and life is very different: Wilde focuses on a youth, Joyce on a family, Wilde on the fading of beauty, Joyce on the interaction of generations.

In 1916 as he was writing the early chapters of *Ulysses* Joyce noted down some of Nora's dreams with his own interpretations. In one of the dreams Nora is fearful that Lucia will be frightened by a newly discovered play of Shakespeare. Joyce's commentary ends, 'The fear for Lucia…is fear that either subsequent honours or the future development of my mind or art or its extravagant excursions into forbidden territory may bring unrest into her life' (*JJ*, 437). Joyce's interpretation is uncannily prescient for Lucia's decline into madness is intimately linked for both father and daughter to *Finnegans Wake*. Nora had, from the beginning, refused to read Joyce's writing and this became, particularly after the publication of *Ulysses*, a major source of conflict. Giorgio also showed no interest in his father's work and early on opted for wine, women, and song as his favourite pursuits. Lucia however was determined to be an artist and for six years she pursued a serious career in modern dance. However, possibly under pressure from both her father and her mother she suddenly abandoned this vocation. Joyce encouraged her to take up graphic design and devoted a considerable amount of his time to drumming up work for her, largely related to his own publishing projects. She also helped her father with *Finnegans Wake*. She was by now showing clear signs of mental illness, which culminated at Joyce's 50th birthday party with a violent attack on her mother. Subsequently her brother Giorgio, to whom she had been devoted, had her confined in a mental hospital for a short period.

For the next three years Joyce dedicated himself to finding a cure for her with repeated stays in mental hospitals and consultations with an endless catalogue of psychiatrists, including Jung. Right from her first episode Giorgio was to argue that permanent institutionalization was the only solution, and after Nora was physically attacked a second time she refused to have Lucia living in the same house. Finally, in 1935, Lucia was admitted to a mental hospital in Ivry, a suburb of Paris. For the three years of Lucia's calvary as she moved between France, England, and Ireland and from one form of captivity to another, Joyce had done little work on what he considered his magnum opus. Now he began to work again furiously six days a week, reserving Sundays for a visit to Lucia in Ivry where they would play the piano and dance. Neither Nora nor Giorgio would accompany him on these visits.

At long last in October 1938 he wrote the final passage of *Finnegans Wake* in one exhausting creative surge. Joyce was pleased enough with Anna Livia's closing monologue that he took it to dinner that night and had it read out loud. His long-time amanuensis Paul Leon was at the table and 'saw that for one of the rare times in their friendship Joyce looked satisfied and proud of himself' (*JJ*, 713). Although there was still rewriting and proofs to be corrected the book begun in 1922 was finished. It would be published on April 1939 just before the long-foreseen outbreak of the Second World War. As Lucia had sunk into madness, Europe had slouched towards war. The thirties had seen a politicization of culture with artists called to take sides, above all on the Spanish Civil War. Although Joyce was to help acquaintances and friends to escape Nazi Germany and although *Finnegans Wake* signals its opposition to any notion of the purity of race or language on every page, Joyce would sign no manifesto nor participate in any congress. To take political sides might limit his readership and, indeed, Joyce's major concern about the forthcoming war was that the publication of his greatest book would go unnoticed. Such was Joyce's stature that *Finnegans Wake* was widely noticed and reviewed but the reviews deeply disappointed the author. Although there was occasional enthusiasm for the linguistic virtuosity few reviewers could make head or tail of its unprecedented experimentalism and even for the well disposed it was a curio.

If the critics have continued to find Joyce's final work impenetrable, the scholars have responded to it magnificently. The first key to *Finnegans Wake* was published in 1944, a mere five years after the *Wake*'s publication, and there have been a multitude of guides and glosses ever since. The most significant work of scholarship has been on the enormous amount of textual material that Joyce generated as he wrote the book. First drafts, word lists, versions published early in *transition* and other magazines, additions to proofs, letters, all of these and more have been subjected to rigorous analysis. Again this work started early with Thomas Connolly's 1961 edition of James Joyce's *Scribbledehobble: The Ur-Workbook of Finnegans Wake* and David Hayman's 1963 edition of *A First Draft Version of Finnegans Wake*.

This work really took off in Paris in the late 1970s, where the theories of writing of the 1960s were joined to new digital tools to produce a genetic criticism which mapped these multitudes of early versions onto the finished text. For three decades this project, which is notable, as is almost all Joycean criticism, for its collective and international nature, has produced what is one of the wonders of modern humanist scholarship. A first stage in this long-term project was marked in 2007 by the multi-authored volume edited by Luca Crispi and Sam Slote, *How Joyce Wrote Finnegans Wake: A Chapter-by-Chapter Genetic Guide*. However it is an inconvenient truth that this magnificent scholarship does not make the *Wake* any easier to read. Indeed even when all the early drafts have yielded up some of the secrets of Joyce's methods, those methods remain largely incomprehensible if one is seeking a hermeneutic key to the book. As Jean-Michel Rabaté, the subtlest of all the Joycean heresiarchs, notes in his contribution to Crispi and Slote's volume, 'The idea of "genetic" approaches to chapters of *Finnegans Wake* is bound to promise more than it can hold' (*HJW*, 384). The whole emphasis of the *Wake* is on the deconstruction of narrative and identity so that any new glimpse of story or self immediately dissolves into the vertiginous whirlpool of the text. This is not to say that these investigations are without interest, indeed they are truly fascinating, but they leave *Finnegans Wake* superbly indifferent.

One of a multitude of fascinating examples: in some of Joyce's preliminary notes about the father's obscure sexual crime there is a sentence derived from the appendix of Frank Harris's biography of Oscar Wilde: 'It is not true that / Pop was homosexual / he had been arrested / at the request of some / nursemaids to whom / he had temporarily / exposed himself / in the Temple gardens'. Harris is challenging accusations that Horatio Lloyd, Wilde's father-in-law, had been suspected of homosexuality: 'The charge against Horatio Lloyd was of a normal kind. It was of exposing himself to nursemaids in the gardens of the Temple' (*HJW*, 9). Harris's sentence does speak volumes about the sexual culture of Joyce's youth and notions of sexual 'normality'. However, the recurring uncertainty of whether the father's obscene crime involved two soldiers or three nursemaids is one element of the *Wake*'s constant refrain of our constitutive bisexuality. The Harris anecdote is of very considerable interest but no anecdote can provide an origin or explanation for a text that refuses both categories.

Joyce is recorded as talking about the *Wake* in two very different registers. On the one hand specific phrases or words are treated as complicated clues in a crossword puzzle in which there really is a meaning to be unlocked. However when he talked more generally of the book the emphasis was on the deepest emotions and the most fundamental levels of our being. The crossword puzzles can as often as not be solved, as we saw in a phrase like 'this Esuan Menshavik'. However, the deeper levels of the text, which Joyce described as a huge mountain which he was boring into at a variety of points in the blind faith that the tunnels would all finally connect, escape even the most learned critics and scholars.

Two years before he finished the *Wake* Joyce talked of what the book meant to him:

> It is a wonderful experience to live with a book. Since 1922 when I began *Work in Progress*, I haven't really lived a normal life. It has required an enormous expenditure of energy. Having written *Ulysses* about the day, I wanted to write this book about the night. Otherwise it has no connection with *Ulysses* and *Ulysses* didn't demand the same expenditure of energy. Since 1922 my book has been a greater reality for me than reality. Everything outside the book has been an insuperable difficulty: the least realities, such as shaving myself in the morning, for example. (*JJ*, 695)

For this last and most complicated of his writings there is no doubt that Joyce found one reader: himself. It is also true that he gathered around him intelligent and convivial helpers: Sylvia Beach, Samuel Beckett, Eugene and Maria Jolas, amongst others, but these helpers could be dismissed by the master at a moment's notice and it is difficult to resist the thought that Joyce's social and intellectual life in Paris is best understood as a cult.

History had deprived him of the audience for which his first three fictions had been written. On 14 January 1922, nineteen days before *Ulysses* was published, the Provisional Government of Ireland was established and the polity in which Joyce had been born and educated and whose passport he carried, the United Kingdom of Britain and Ireland, ceased to be. While Joyce continued to welcome any visitors from Ireland who beat their way to his Parisian lairs and to quiz them about his native land, there are no records of him taking sides in the debate on the treaty that had established that independent government, although that treaty continued to be the dominant topic of political discussion in Ireland until his death.

Joyce had held from early on that opposition to English rule was pointless while the Catholic Church tyrannized hearts and minds. For Joyce the Irish Free State was not a step forward but a step back from English rule as the Catholic Church became *de facto* if not *de jure* the ruler of the Irish Free State. One of his few recorded comments on the new nation is scathing: 'In the Dublin of my day there was the kind of desperate freedom which comes from a lack of responsibility, for the English were in governance then, so everyone said what he liked. Now I hear that since the Free State came in there is less freedom. The Church has made inroads everywhere, so that we are in fact becoming a bourgeois nation, with the Church supplying the aristocracy...and I do not see much hope for us intellectually. Once the Church is in command she will devour everything...what she will leave will be a few old rags not worth the having: and we may degenerate to the position of a second Spain' (*Conv.*, 65). The depth of Joyce's rejection of the new nation of Ireland is astonishing. In November 1940 Joyce and his family had fled German-occupied Paris and were desperately seeking visas that would enable them, and Lucia, to find refuge in Switzerland. They were in danger of internment and worse. All of their problems could have been instantly solved by availing themselves of Irish passports which would have rendered them non-combatants. Joyce rejected such a solution (*JJ*, 738).

One of the paradoxes of *Finnegans Wake* is that it attempts to subvert the historical dominance of language and literature entirely in linguistic form and literary medium. In his reflections on history in the second chapter of *Ulysses*, Stephen meditates on the status of possible futures that did not come to pass: 'But can those have been possible seeing that they never were? Or was that

94

only possible that came to pass?' (*U*, 30). The crucial event which determined the form of Ireland's national liberation was the European Civil War, which began in August 1914. If instead we were to imagine a European Revolution which gave birth to a secular and socialist Irish republic, it would be possible to imagine a multimedia production of *Finnegans Wake* at the Abbey Theatre in which the dancing of Lucia Joyce played a central role.

In reality all we have is a book full of linguistic invention and literary innovation whose solitary and isolated origins deprives it of any general readership.

And yet. And yet. Were I to be asked to nominate one sequence from Joyce for inclusion in an anthology of English writing to be published in the year 3000, it would not be the final sequence of 'The Dead', nor the Christmas dinner argument over Parnell, nor even one of the interior monologues of *Ulysses*. The finest and most moving prose that I know in English is the final sequence of *Finnegans Wake* which begins 'Soft morning, city!' (*FW*, 619). The passage that Joyce had listened to with such pleasure in October 1938 was expanded but unlike almost all of the rest of *Finnegans Wake* the expansion did not overcomplicate the references and, even more unusually, left syntax and lexis simple. From early on Joyce had seen his mad book and his mad daughter in some kind of mystic correspondence and in the final years harboured the belief that when he finished his book, Lucia would finish her madness. This may speak to the extraordinary emotional charge of the final words of the book which enacts Anna Livia's final descent into the sea of death:

> First we feel. Then we fall. And let her rain now if she likes. Gently
> or strongly as she likes. Anyway let her rain for my time is come.
> I done me best when I was let. Thinking always if I go all goes.
> A hundred cares, a tithe of troubles and is there one who
> understands me? One in a thousand of years of the nights? All me
> life I have been lived among them but now they are becoming

lothed to me. And I am lothing their little warm tricks. And lothing
their mean cosy turns. And all the greedy gushes out through their
small souls. And all the lazy leaks down over their brash bodies.
How small it's all! And me letting on to meself always. And lilting
on all the time. I thought you were all glittering with the noblest of
carriage. You're only a bumpkin. I thought you the great in all
things, in guilt and in glory. You're but a puny. Home! My people
were not their sort out beyond there so far as I can. For all the bold
and bad and bleary they are blamed, the seahags. No! Nor for all
our wild dances in all their wild din. I can seen meself among them,
allaniuvia pulchrabelled. How she was handsome, the wild Amazia,
when she would seize to my other breast! And what is she weird,
haughty Niluna, that she will snatch from my ownest hair! For 'tis
they are the stormies. Ho hang! Hang ho! And the clash of our cries
till we spring to be free. Auravoles, they says, never heed of your
name! But I'm loothing them that's here and all I lothe. Loonely in
me loneness. For all their faults. I am passing out. O bitter ending!
I'll slip away before they're up. They'll never see. Nor know. Nor
miss me. And it's old and old it's sad and old it's sad and weary I go
back to you, my cold father, my cold mad father, my cold mad feary
father, till the near sight of the mere size of him, the moyles and
moyles of it, moananoaning, makes me seasilt saltsick and I rush,
my only, into your arms. I see them rising! Save me from those
therrble prongs! Two more. Onetwo moremens more. So. Avelaval.
My leaves have drifted from me. All. But one clings still. I'll bear it
on me. To remind me of. Lff! So soft this morning, ours. Yes. Carry
me along, taddy, like you done through the toy fair! If I seen him
bearing down on me now under whitespread wings like he'd come
from Arkangels, I sink I'd die down over his feet, humbly dumbly,
only to washup. Yes, tid. There's where. First. We pass through grass
behush the bush to. Whish! A gull. Gulls. Far calls. Coming, far!
End here. Us then. Finn, again! Take. Bussoftlhee, mememormee!
Till thousendsthee. Lps. The keys to. Given! A way a lone a last a
loved a long the. (*FW*, 627–8)

Chapter 6
The Aunt Josephine Paradox

In January 1965 I was 15 and staying for the last part of my Christmas holidays in Kilkenny. My bedroom belonged to the youngest son of the house. He was a law student in Dublin but on his bedside table was *A Portrait of the Artist as a Young Man*. I started the book at bedtime and read it all through the night. The text was fully contemporary. Joyce was not writing about the past but about the present, about the conflict between sex and religion which is endemic to Catholicism and which is the defining feature of the form that developed in Ireland after the Reformation as the native inhabitants adopted allegiance to the see of Rome as the most effective way of marking their repudiation of the English colonizers.

In May 2015 a referendum was held in the Republic of Ireland to amend the constitution by adding the stipulation that marriage is recognized irrespective of the sex of the partners. The proposed amendment received more than 60 per cent of the vote and the amendment was signed into law on 29 August 2015 by the President of Ireland as the Thirty-Fourth Amendment of the constitution. Other countries had already legalized same-sex marriages but Ireland became the first country in the world to define marriage in its constitution as a relationship indifferent to sex. There can be little doubt that one of the shades who blessed this astonishing development was James Augustine Joyce, the great Irish bard of polymorphously perverse sexuality. The shade may also have felt a hint of regret that the Ireland which had made him was passing away for this vote was one of the final developments of a radical transformation of the country of his birth which saw the rejection of the authority of the Roman Catholic Church.

In whatever world Joyce now exists he can also have taken real pride in the role that his first novel had played in maintaining an unwavering hostility to the Catholic Church. Throughout the period that the Church effectively ruled Ireland after independence in 1922, *A Portrait* maintained an important dissenting voice, which asserted realities of flesh and spirit that the Catholic Church was unable to acknowledge. *A Portrait* also insisted that to be Irish was to be European. In doing so it took direct aim against the insular nationalism which was to take power after the War of Independence. There is no doubt that Joyce would have rejoiced in 1973 when Ireland joined the European Economic Community. Joyce knew that he was an Irish writer but he aspired to become a European one.

In fact he outdid his own aspirations for *A Portrait*'s appeal is not merely European but international. When I meet my freshman students each year in Pittsburgh I know that the only non-American novel they are likely to have read is *A Portrait*. Its appeal is not limited by nationality or even religion. Joyce's account of the growth of an individual soul and body in opposition to the authorities who demand vows of obedience continues to reach audiences of contemporary American teenagers.

Forecasting the future of literary reputation is a fool's errand. In the 1660s most educated readers would have agreed that Abraham Cowley was the greatest of English poets; I doubt that many readers of this book have even heard Cowley's name. But if we cannot read into the future we can make an accounting of a book which has been in print for over 100 years. Joyce ends

A Portrait with the promise to forge the conscience of his race and who can deny that the Irish voters who opted to join Europe in 1973 or to write marriage without distinction of sex into the constitution in 2015 had consciences which, whether they had read Joyce or not, had been partially formed by *A Portrait of the Artist as a Young Man*.

A Portrait was hailed as a masterpiece on publication. *Dubliners* had a quieter start. Reviews were respectful and the book was classed as simple naturalism. It continued to be read as a prentice work until well after Joyce's death. In the past few decades, however, it has been recognized as the masterpiece that it is. One can indicate some of the stepping-stones in this process. In 1986, as he approached death, the legendary American filmmaker John Huston determined to make a final film, an adaptation of 'The Dead'. Although he died before the film was released in 1987, Huston made sure that his homage to Joyce was a masterpiece which garnered both popular and critical acclaim. All the performances are stunning but Huston's daughter Angelica embodies Gretta Conroy with a grace and accuracy which defies superlatives. By the time the film was released *Dubliners* had also gained ground in courses on the short story and had become a much taught text.

This teaching led to more and more careful reading and the secondary literature on *Dubliners* has become richer and richer. If one was to pick out one jewel amongst many it would be Margot Norris's *Suspicious Readings of Joyce's Dubliners*, published in 2003. The final canonization of Joyce's early work came from Ian McEwan, one of England's pre-eminent novelists, in a blog devoted to the novella in the *New Yorker* on 29 October 2012:

> The great novella is Joyce's 'The Dead.' A simple binary structure
> (a party, a hotel room) supports the evocation of an entire social
> milieu (decorous and fractious by turns) with extraordinary
> warmth. They seem to play out in real time, the dancing and

singing at the aunts' annual dinner, the family tensions, the barbed exchange about national identity. Then Gabriel and Gretta's exchange in their hotel room, the muted drama of his disappointed ardor, her piercingly sad revelation of a boy who once loved her and died, and, at last, Gabriel's final, drowsy, shamed reflections on his own lovelessness, and on mortality, prompted by memories of the evening's merrymaking—these are among the most exquisite passages of prose fiction in the entire canon.

These considerations might make it seem easy to class Joyce as amongst the greatest of writers in English but these were the works of his youth and his later works pose distinctive problems. *Ulysses* is very widely recognized as one of the greatest novels of the 20th century. Many, myself included, would count it as the greatest. There is however a major problem. *Ulysses* is spectacularly difficult to read. It dispenses with most of the cues that we expect in a work of fiction and it changes styles and perspectives in bewildering fashion. There are some who read this difficulty as the stratagem of an elite author attempting to drum up a profitable subscription list. It must be said that those who put forward such theories have neither read Joyce's work with any attention nor studied his life with even a minimum of empathy. Joyce is fundamentally committed to the virtues of the everyday.

This does not mean that he did not spend an inordinate amount of time cultivating his reputation. The collective text on *Work in Progress* published in 1929 bore a title *Our Exagmination Round his Factification for Incamination of* Work in Progress, and included contributions from Samuel Beckett and William Carlos Williams, who would themselves become major modernist writers. Having secured his avant-garde wing Joyce then encouraged and partly dictated Stuart Gilbert's *James Joyce's Ulysses: A Study*. Gilbert was a brilliant linguist, a serious classical scholar, and deeply versed in Indian thought. Gilbert makes of *Ulysses* a book deeply grounded in Homeric scholarship and spiritualism. Both the modernist collective and the individual classicist pay all but no attention to post-Renaissance European culture. Exceptions are made for Giordano Bruno and Giambattista Vico but these exceptions are marginal to the dominant European tradition. Joyce is seen as both a complete and revolutionary break with the past and a continuation of the most ancient of world cultures. He is not however placed in the tradition of elite European culture.

This is what repelled both Virginia Woolf and Erich Auerbach, the great German critic. Woolf in her diary for 16 August 1922 recorded of *Ulysses*, 'An illiterate, underbred book it seems to me: the book of a self-taught working man, & we all know how distressing they are, how egotistic, insistent, raw, striking, & ultimately nauseating.' Auerbach in the closing pages of his masterpiece *Mimesis* used slightly more moderate language but similar sentiments when he called *Ulysses* a 'mocking hodgepodge...of the European tradition' (*Mim.*, 551). What English lady and Prussian Jew both saw clearly was that, far from addressing a traditional elite audience, Joyce was determined to ignore both tradition and audience. For Joyce as an Irishman there was no European tradition from the moment that Elizabeth launched total war both military and cultural on the Irish and their language, a war intensified and completed by Oliver Cromwell. While Joyce has a fierce allegiance to Ibsen and the Europe that he represents, it is to a writer and a continent which is breaking with its bourgeois history. The cultural commonality that Woolf and Auerbach automatically share has no resonance for Joyce at all.

For Joyce, the Irishman, the European tradition is a tradition of oppression and violence to which the First World War is the inevitable conclusion rather than a distressing aberration. In attempting to produce a book which would celebrate both the ordinary and the peaceful, and play its part in ushering in a celebration of the democratic, Joyce was forced to deconstruct the fundamentals of Western European culture. This deconstruction makes *Ulysses* anything but a democratic book for it requires a knowledge of the elite culture that is being held up for scorn and ridicule. This was borne in on Joyce in the most painful way when he sent a copy of *Ulysses* to Josephine Murray, his mother's sister. Aunt Josephine was the woman in Ireland to whom he was closest. A favourite since childhood, it was she who had offered consolation when his mother died, it was to her that he confided all the initial problems of his relationship with Nora.

She complained that she found the book incomprehensible and Joyce, who had already told her to read Homer's *Odyssey*, wrote in a letter of 10 November 1922 that she should now try '*The Adventures of Ulysses* (which is Homer's story told in simple English much abbreviated) by Charles Lamb. You can read it in a night and can buy it at Gill's or Browne and Nolan's for a couple of shillings. Then have a try at *Ulysses* again' (*Letters I*, 193). The letter provides perhaps the most telling example—there are others—of the fact that Joyce hoped for a very general readership and underestimated wildly the difficulties that *Ulysses* posed the reader. These difficulties, it must be said, are not specific to Joyce; they are common to all those modernist texts which, as Auerbach wrote, 'put the emphasis on the random occurrence, to exploit it not in the service of a planned continuity of action but in itself. And in the process something new and elemental appeared: nothing less than the wealth of reality and depth of life in every moment to which we surrender ourselves without prejudice' (*Mim.*, 552).

It is this surrender without prejudice which is the difficulty of these modernist texts and which means that, as in Woolf and Eliot, Joyce's commitment to the democratization of experience necessarily involves a more direct encounter with the process of writing than is offered by the Western literary tradition. What one might call the Aunt Josephine paradox is a feature not just of Joyce's *Ulysses* but of all the great modernist texts up to and including Salman Rushdie's *The Satanic Verses* and Zadie

Smith's *NW*. Our understanding of this paradox may yet develop. I have argued that Joyce's attention to writing as a medium was a result of the emergence of cinema as a completely new medium which in its direct representation of reality involved no intervening consciousness. But the media proliferate and the games industry is now bigger than the movie and the music business combined. Whether these media developments will render the experiment of modernism a dead end, when the idea of the writer broke against the democratic public, or whether it will become the beginning of a universal illumination may still be in doubt. What is certain is that *Ulysses* will retain its position as one of the greatest novels of the 20th century, whether it is read as end or beginning.

However, Joyce was less interested in the critical fate of *Ulysses* than of his last book to which he devoted seventeen years (*Ulysses* had taken a mere seven). After Joyce died Nora Barnacle would get irritated with visitors who wanted to talk about *Ulysses*, insisting that the great book was *Finnegans Wake*. I have indicated that whatever its achievements *Finnegans Wake* is in Joyce's own terms a failure but I would like to end with two wild speculations which might render my own judgement null and void.

In the whole of the English literary tradition it is difficult to find any writer whose command of the sounds of the English language is so profound. Shakespeare and Pope are the only competitors of which I am aware. A good example can be found in the very first lines in which we encounter Leopold Bloom and his cat. It is conventional in English to represent a cat's mewing sound with 'Miaow', which is the word that Bloom uses when he addresses the cat later in the chapter (55). But when the cat speaks on the first page Joyce transcribes it as 'Mkgnao' (45). The use of gutturals and nasals gives the cat's typical cry that hint of aggression which is lost in the conventional 'Miaow'. Joyce emphasizes this when later on the same page he adds the very pronounced r, which is peculiar and specific to Hiberno English, to the cat's increasingly impassioned cries for attention. This not only throws a burr into the phonetic mix of the cacophonous Miaow but gives Bloom's cat an Irish accent. Joyce's astonishing grasp of the sounds of English, honed as a language teacher in multilingual Trieste, is a feature of his first three books. It may be, however, that a thorough phonetic analysis of *Finnegans Wake* would finally make that extraordinary work sing.

There is, however, a more recent development which might be even more pregnant with possibility. In 2013 a translation of *Finnegans Wake* was published in Shanghai and shot to the top of the best-seller lists, outpacing even Ian McEwan's *Atonement*. The translator says that eventually there will be two translations: the first is devoted to lexical accuracy, the second will apply Joyce's method to the Chinese ideograms themselves. On its publication the translator Congrong Dai said, '*Finnegans Wake* is a book of freedom. I do not only mean political freedom. Joyce will create new words to transcend social restraints. So the making of a new word shows Joyce's disobedience.'

Joyce's final work finds beginnings in endings and endings in beginning. The closing sentences of the book which focus on endings are interrupted by the hailing of another beginning which perhaps foreshadows the book's life in Chinese. Finn, again! (*FW*, 628)

Further reading

Joyce has some claim to be the most commented-on writer in Modern English. The *James Joyce Quarterly* receives 150 new items of criticism and scholarship each quarter. A full bibliography would fill many volumes of this size. This bibliography is divided into three sections:

A chapter-by-chapter annotated bibliography of the books that have been most important for this text

A brief bibliography of Joyce's works

A guide to further bibliographies and scholarly tools which will enable the interested reader to navigate the vast oceans of Joyce scholarship and criticism

Chapter-by-Chapter Annotated Bibliographies

Chapter 1: A publication in post-First World War Paris

Anderson, Margaret. *My Thirty Years War*. New York: Covici, Friede, 1930. The memoirs of one of the American publishers of *Ulysses* who risked imprisonment by publishing episodes of the novel in *The Little Review*.

Beach, Sylvia. *Shakespeare and Company*. New York: Harcourt Brace, 1959. Sylvia Beach and her bookshop Shakespeare and Company offered Joyce constant support in his first decade in Paris. This book chronicles their relationship in the context of Beach's famous bookshop.

Birmingham, Kevin. *The Most Dangerous Book: The Battle for James Joyce's* Ulysses. New York: Penguin, 2014. Brilliant historical analysis of the obstacles facing Joyce in both publishing and distributing *Ulysses*.

Byrne, J. F. *Silent Years: An Autobiography with Memoirs of James Joyce and Our Ireland*. New York: Farrar, Strauss and Young, 1953. Byrne (Cranly in *A Portrait*) was Joyce's closest friend in Dublin, counselling him in 1904 before he left Dublin with Nora and in 1909 when Cosgrave (Lynch in *A Portrait*) claimed Nora had been unfaithful. Ellmann's description is as follows: 'Byrne wrote a memoir, largely about Joyce, in which he made clear that he was withholding more information than he was furnishing, added a coded appendix to it, and gave the whole the appropriate title of *Silent Years*. It is one of the most crotchety and interesting of the many books of Joyce's friends.'

Colum, Mary and Padraic. *Our Friend James Joyce*. New York: Doubleday, 1958. The Colums were lifelong friends of Joyce (Padraic met Joyce when he was a student) and this memoir covers a friendship which lasted to the very end.

Curran, C. P. *James Joyce Remembered*. Oxford: Oxford University Press, 1968. Interesting set of reactions to Joyce's depiction of Dublin from a student friend who stayed in the city of their birth.

Ellmann, Richard. *James Joyce* (2nd edition). Oxford: Oxford University Press, 1982. The indispensable biography. Some errors, some misperceptions, but a tremendous scholarly achievement.

Gorman, Herbert. *James Joyce*. New York: Farrar and Rinehart, 1948. Gorman's biography, although full of errors dictated by Joyce, is fascinating as a record of how Joyce wanted to present himself to the world in the 1930s.

Joyce, Stanislaus. *The Dublin Diary of Stanislaus Joyce*. Edited by George Harris. Ithaca, NY: Cornell University Press, 1962. Not particularly focused on James Joyce (the elopement with Nora is not recorded until long after the event) but a vivid picture of the Joyce household and Dublin at the turn of the century.

Maddox, Brenda. *Nora: The Real Life of Molly Bloom*. Boston: Houghton Mifflin, 1988. This biography of Nora Barnacle is a tremendous complement to Ellmann's life, written by a journalist with an eye for the story.

Pound, Ezra. *Pound/Joyce: The Letters of Ezra Pound to James Joyce*. Edited by Forrest Read. London: Faber and Faber, 1967. Pound wrote a very good letter and if you don't mind the American demotic this is a fascinating record of relations between Pound and Joyce over three decades.

Power, Arthur. *Conversations with James Joyce*. Edited by Clive Hart. New York: Barnes and Noble, 1974. Power was an Irish painter and art critic in Paris who talked often with Joyce on a wide variety of topics. He wrote down some of what they discussed as Joyce finished *Ulysses* and this is a record of Joyce's table talk when he had given up all journalism.

Chapter 2: *Dubliners*

Gifford, Don, and Robert J. Seidman. *Notes for Joyce: Dubliners and a Portrait of the Artist*. New York: E. P. Dutton, 1967. A useful aid to reading both *Dubliners* and *A Portrait*.

Joyce, Stanislaus. *My Brother's Keeper: James Joyce's Early Years*. Edited by Richard Ellmann. London: Faber and Faber, 1958. Stanislaus's unfortunately unfinished memoir about his brother who he both idolized and resented. Full of information about Joyce's early years.

Kenner, Hugh. *Dublin's Joyce*. Bloomington: Indiana University Press, 1956. Kenner's original analysis of Eveline was articulated in this critical analysis of all of Joyce's work.

Mahaffey, Vicki, ed. *Collaborative Dubliners: Joyce in Dialogue*. Syracuse, NY: Syracuse University Press, 2012. Each story of *Dubliners* commented on by two eminent Joyceans in dialogue. A festival of criticism which owes much to Margot Norris's (herself a contributor) 2003 book.

Mullin, Katherine. 'Don't Cry for me, Argentina: "Eveline" and the Seductions of Emigration Propaganda'. In *Semicolonial Joyce*, edited by Derek Attridge and Marjorie Howes, 172–200. New York: Cambridge University Press, 2000. Brilliant historical investigation of the place of Argentina in the reality and fantasy of emigration in 1904 Ireland and England.

Norris, Margot. *Suspicious Readings of Joyce's Dubliners*. Philadelphia: University of Pennsylvania Press, 2003. Dazzling, detailed readings of all of the stories of *Dubliners*. The one indispensable book of criticism on *Dubliners*.

Chapter 3: *A Portrait*

Deane, Seamus. 'Introduction'. In *A Portrait of the Artist as a Young Man*, edited by Seamus Deane. London: Penguin, 1992. A magisterial placing of *A Portrait* in its social and historical setting.

Gifford, Don, and Robert J. Seidman. *Notes for Joyce: Dubliners and a Portrait of the Artist*. New York: E. P. Dutton, 1967. Valuable annotations.

Mahon, Peter. *James Joyce: A Guide for the Perplexed*. London: Continuum, 2009. This very good book has a particularly brilliant second chapter on *A Portrait*.

Scholes, Robert, and Richard M. Kain, eds. *The Workshop of Daedalus*. Evanston, Ill.: Northwestern University Press, 1965. Indispensable collection of Joyce's early unpublished writings together with useful contextual material.

Staley, Thomas F., and Bernard Benstock, eds. *Approaches to Joyce's Portrait: Ten Essays*. Pittsburgh: University of Pittsburgh Press, 1976. Good collection of earlier criticism. Hans Walter Gabler's textual history of *A Portrait* is particularly useful.

Valente, Joseph. 'Thrilled by His Touch: Homosexual Panic and the Will to Artistry in A Portrait of the Artist as a Young Man'. *James Joyce Quarterly* 31, no. 3 (Spring 1994): 167–88. Uses, to considerable effect, Eve Sedgwick's categories to analyse the homosexual threads in *A Portrait*. See also the longer version of this article in Joseph Valente, ed. *Quare Joyce*. Ann Arbor: University of Michigan Press, 1998.

Wollaeger, Mark A., ed. *James Joyce's A Portrait of the Artist as a Young Man: A Casebook*. New York: Oxford University Press, 2003. An excellent collection of more modern criticism.

Chapter 4: *Ulysses*

Budgen, Frank. *James Joyce and the Making of Ulysses*. London: Grayson and Grayson, 1934. Tremendous account of Joyce at work by his best friend in Zurich, the painter Frank Budgen.

Ellmann, Maud. '"Penelope" without the Body'. *European Joyce Studies* 17 (2006): 97–108. A fascinating and compelling account of Penelope from one of the most acute of Joycean readers.

Ellmann, Richard. *Ulysses on the Liffey*. London: Faber and Faber, 1972. Joyce's most important biographer produces a liberal humanist reading of Joyce, full of learning and illumination.

Gibson, Andrew. *Joyce's Revenge: History, Politics and Aesthetics in Ulysses*. Oxford: Oxford University Press, 2002. Elucidates Joyce's novel with detailed historical and political context.

Gilbert, Stuart. *James Joyce's Ulysses: A Study*. London: Faber and Faber, 1930. This is the first book-length study of Joyce's novel, much of it semi-dictated by the master. Gilbert is particularly good on Homer and on Berard's study which so informed Joyce. He is also good on spiritualism; a major influence on Joyce and his book but not on more modern critics.

Kiberd, Declan. *Ulysses and Us: The Art of Everyday Living*. London: Faber and Faber, 2009. An impassioned plea for *Ulysses* as a democratic work of art. Fine local readings and real commitment to a popular *Ulysses*. Also useful contexts from Irish literature. Kiberd's introduction to his Penguin edition of *Ulysses* is perhaps the best short introduction to Joyce's novel.

MacCabe, Colin. *James Joyce and the Revolution of the Word*. 2nd edn. London: Macmillan, 2003. This book uses the theories of language of Jacques Derrida and Jacques Lacan to produce a political reading of Joyce. Although many local insights and interpretations are valuable (and I have used some lightly in this chapter) the framing Leninist argument is wrong and rebarbative.

McCourt, John. *The Years of Bloom: James Joyce in Trieste, 1904–1920*. Dublin: The Lilliput Press, 2000. Magnificent demonstration of how central Trieste was to Joyce's development as a writer.

Norris, Margot. *Virgin and Veteran Readings of Ulysses*. New York: Palgrave Macmillan, 2017. A series of marvellously enlightening close readings including, very rare in the extensive Joyce bibliography, serious consideration of Stephen's anti-Semitic ballad in Ithaca.

Further reading

Senn, Fritz. 'Righting *Ulysses*'. In *James Joyce: New Perspectives*, edited by Colin MacCabe, 3–28. Brighton: The Harvester Press, 1982. Fritz Senn is the greatest of Joyce scholars and all his work repays close attention. This essay is a perfect introduction to Joyce's verbal strategies in *Ulysses*.

Thornton, Weldon. *Allusions in Ulysses: An Annotated List*. Chapel Hill, NC: University of North Carolina Press, 1968. An indispensable guide.

Trotter, David. *Cinema and Modernism*. Malden: Blackwell, 2007. A brilliant reading of the centrality of the new medium of cinema to the development of modernist writing in Woolf, Eliot, and Joyce. The most sophisticated reading of André Bazin in English.

Chapter 5: *Finnegans Wake*

Attridge, Derek. 'Finnegans Awake: The Dream of Interpretation'. *James Joyce Quarterly* 50, no. 1/2 (Fall 1989): 11–29. Forensic analysis of notions of dream and dreamer in *Finnegans Wake* and its critics.

Bishop, John. *Joyce's Book of the Dark*. Madison: University of Wisconsin Press, 1986. Brilliant and scholarly reading of Joyce's book as a book of the night.

Connolly, Thomas E., ed. *James Joyce's Scribbledehobble: The Ur Workbook for Finnegans Wake*. Evanston, Ill.: Northwestern University Press, 1961. One of the important notebooks that Joyce put together in his early preparations for *Finnegans Wake*.

Crispi, Luca, and Sam Slote, eds. *How Joyce Wrote Finnegans Wake: A Chapter by Chapter Genetic Guide*. Madison: University of Wisconsin Press, 2007. Magisterial guide to the varieties of genetic criticism of the *Wake*.

Hayman, David. *A First-Draft Version of Finnegans Wake*. Austin: University of Texas Press, 1963. An exceptionally useful redaction of the 9,000 pages of notes and drafts held in the British Museum.

Heath, Stephen. 'Ambiviolences: Notes for Reading Joyce'. In *Post-Structuralist Joyce: Essays from the French*, edited by Derek Attridge and Daniel Ferrer, 31–66. Cambridge: Cambridge University Press, 1984. Powerful reading of Joyce and particularly *Finnegans Wake* in terms of French theory of the 1960s.

MacCabe, Colin. 'An Introduction to *Finnegans Wake*'. In *James Joyce's Finnegans Wake: A Casebook*, edited by John Harty, 22–32. New York: Garland, 1991. The first half of this chapter draws very heavily on this earlier introduction.

McHugh, Roland. *Annotations to Finnegans Wake* (3rd edn). Baltimore: Johns Hopkins University Press, 2006. Indispensable guide.

Platt, Len. *Joyce, Race and Finnegans Wake*. Cambridge: Cambridge University Press, 2007. A thorough investigation of *Finnegans Wake* as an attack on notions of race.

Shloss, Carol Loeb. *Lucia Joyce: To Dance in the Wake*. London: Bloomsbury, 2004. Full of interesting information and less interesting psychology.

Chapter 6: The Aunt Josephine Paradox

Barry, Kevin. *The Dead*. Cork: Cork University Press, 2001. Brilliant and subtle reading of Joyce's story and Huston's film, which also traces the relations between *The Dead* and Rossellini's masterpiece *Viaggio in Italia*.

MacCabe, Colin. *Perpetual Carnival: Essays on Film and Literature*. New York: Oxford University Press, 2017. Part 1 of this book ('Modernism') develops in more detail the general argument about modernism sketched in this chapter. These arguments also inform the beginning of the chapter on *Ulysses*.

A Brief Bibliography of Joyce's Works

In the past decades there have been many new editions including a
   mammoth undertaking by Hans Gabler which, aside from
   providing much mirth, proved definitively that there is no
   definitive text of *Ulysses*.

A full discussion of the arguments over the Gabler edition can be
   found in Charles Rossman, 'The Critical Reception of the "Gabler
   Ulysses": Or, Gabler's *Ulysses* Kidd-napped', *Studies in the Novel*
   21, no. 2 (Summer 1989): 154–81; and Mark Wollaeger, '*Ulysses*,
   Gabler, and Kidd: The Personal Note', *Studies in the Novel* 51, no. 1
   (Spring 2019): 86–97.

My choice of the editions of Joyce's major works used in this book was
   determined by their introductions and notes.

Books published in Joyce's lifetime (in chronological order by original date of publication)

Chamber Music. London: Elkin Matthews, 1907.

Dubliners. London: Grant Richards Ltd., 1914.

A Portrait of the Artist as a Young Man. New York:
   B. W. Huebsch, 1916.

Exiles: A Play in Three Acts. London: Grant Richards, 1918.

Ulysses. Paris: Shakespeare and Company, 1922.

Pomes Penyeach. Paris: Shakespeare and Company, 1927.

Collected Poems. New York: Black Sun Press, 1936.

Finnegans Wake. London: Faber and Faber, 1939.

Writings published after Joyce's death (in chronological order roughly corresponding to the date of original composition)

Occasional, Critical, and Political Writings. Edited by Kevin Barry.
   Oxford: Oxford University Press, 2000.

Stephen Hero. Edited by Theodore Spencer, John J. Slocum, and
   Herbert Cahoon. New York: New Directions, 1955.

'Manuscript Materials'. In *The Workshop of Daedalus: James Joyce
   and the Raw Materials for A Portrait of the Artist as a Young Man*,
   edited by Robert Scholes and Richard M. Kain, 3–108. Evanston,
   Ill.: Northwestern University Press, 1965.

Giacomo Joyce. Edited by Richard Ellmann. London: Faber and
   Faber, 1968.

James Joyce in Padua. Edited by Louis Berrone. New York: Random
   House, 1977. [Examination essays from 1912]

Joyce and Hauptmann: Before Sunrise: James Joyce's Translation.
Edited by Jill Perkins. San Marino: Henry E. Huntington Library
and Art Gallery, 1978.

James Joyce's Letters to Sylvia Beach, 1921-1940. Edited by Melissa
Banta and Oscar A. Silverman. Bloomington: Indiana University
Press, 1987.

The Cat and the Devil. London: Faber and Faber, 1965.

Poems and Shorter Writings. Edited by Richard Ellmann. London:
Faber and Faber, 1991.

Poems and Exiles. Edited by J. C. C. Mays. London: Penguin, 1992.

Letters. Edited by Stuart Gilbert [vol. 1] and Richard Ellmann [vols.
2–3]. London: Faber and Faber, 1957–66.

Selected Letters. Edited by Richard Ellmann. London: Faber and
Faber, 1975.

*The Joyce Calendar: Published, Unpublished, and Ungathered
Correspondence by James Joyce* (online resource). Edited by
William S. Brockman. <norman.hrc.utexas.edu/jamesjoycechecklist/
calendar.cfm>

Manuscript photoreproductions and transcriptions (in chronological order by date of publication)

Joyce's Ulysses *Notesheets in the British Museum.* Edited by
Phillip F. Herring. Charlottesville: Bibliographic Society of the
University of Virginia, 1972. [Joyce's notes]

Ulysses: A Facsimile of the Manuscript. Edited by Clive Driver. 3 vols.
London: Faber and Faber, 1975.

Joyce's Notes and Early Drafts for Ulysses*: Selections from the Buffalo
Collection.* Edited by Phillip F. Herring. Charlottesville:
Bibliographic Society of the University of Virginia, 1977. [Notes for
Ulysses and early drafts of 'Cyclops' and 'Circe']

The James Joyce Archive. Michael Groden (General Editor), Hans
Walter Gabler, David Hayman, A. Walton Litz, and Danis Rose
(Associate Editors). 63 vols. New York: Garland Publishing, 1977–9.

The Finnegans Wake Notebooks at Buffalo. Edited by Vincent Deane,
Daniel Ferrer, and Geert Lernout. 12 vols to date. 2001–.

A Guide to Further Bibliographies and Study Tools

Bibliographies (in chronological order by date of publication)

Slocum, John J., and Herbert Cahoon, eds. *A Bibliography of James
Joyce, 1882-1941.* London: R. Hart-Davis, 1953. [primary]

Deming, Robert H. *A Bibliography of James Joyce Studies* (2nd edition). Boston: G. K. Hall, 1977.

Rice, Thomas Jackson. *James Joyce: A Guide to Research*. New York: Garland, 1982. [annotated]

Staley, Thomas F. *An Annotated Critical Bibliography of James Joyce*. New York: Harvester Wheatsheaf, 1989. [annotated]

The James Joyce Checklist Online (online resource). Edited by William S. Brockman. <https://norman.hrc.utexas.edu/ JamesJoyceChecklist/index.cfm>. Undoubtedly the single most comprehensive online bibliography. The Checklist is a compilation of the entire *James Joyce Quarterly* checklist, updated every quarter. It can be searched by keyword, topic, title, etc., and is the single most useful (and most used) digital bibliography available.

Journals

James Joyce Review. 1957–9.

A Wake Newslitter. 1962–80, plus 1982–4.

James Joyce Quarterly. 1963–.

James Joyce Broadsheet. 1980–.

A 'Finnegans Wake' Circular. 1985–.

James Joyce Literary Supplement. 1987–.

Joyce Studies Annual. 1990–2004, 2007–.

Hypermedia Joyce Studies. 1996, plus 1998– [online].

Genetic Joyce Studies. 2001– [online].

Index

For the benefit of digital users, indexed terms that span two pages (e.g., 52–53) may, on occasion, appear on only one of those pages.

BESTSELLERS
A Very Short Introduction
John Sutherland

'I rejoice', said Doctor Johnson, 'to concur with the Common Reader.' For the last century, the tastes and preferences of the common reader have been reflected in the American and British bestseller lists, and this *Very Short Introduction* takes an engaging look through the lists to reveal what we have been reading - and why. John Sutherland shows that bestseller lists monitor one of the strongest pulses in modern literature and are therefore worthy of serious study. Along the way, he lifts the lid on the bestseller industry, examines what makes a book into a bestseller, and asks what separates bestsellers from canonical fiction.

'His amiable trawl through the history of popular books is frequently entertaining'

Scott Pack, The Times

ENGLISH LITERATURE
A Very Short Introduction
Jonathan Bate

Sweeping across two millennia and every literary genre, acclaimed scholar and biographer Jonathan Bate provides a dazzling introduction to English Literature. The focus is wide, shifting from the birth of the novel and the brilliance of English comedy to the deep Englishness of landscape poetry and the ethnic diversity of Britain's Nobel literature laureates. It goes on to provide a more in-depth analysis, with close readings from an extraordinary scene in King Lear to a war poem by Carol Ann Duffy, and a series of striking examples of how literary texts change as they are transmitted from writer to reader.

{No reviews}

www.oup.com/vsi

WRITING AND SCRIPT
A Very Short Introduction
Andrew Robinson

Without writing, there would be no records, no history, no books, and no emails. Writing is an integral and essential part of our lives; but when did it start? Why do we all write differently and how did writing develop into what we use today? All of these questions are answered in this *Very Short Introduction*. Starting with the origins of writing five thousand years ago, with cuneiform and Egyptian hieroglyphs, Andrew Robinson explains how these early forms of writing developed into hundreds of scripts including the Roman alphabet and the Chinese characters.

'User-friendly survey.'

Steven Poole, The Guardian

www.oup.com/vsi

CATHOLICISM
A Very Short Introduction
Gerald O'Collins

Despite a long history of external threats and internal strife, the Roman Catholic Church and the broader reality of Catholicism remain a vast and valuable presence into the third millennium of world history. What are the origins of the Catholic Church? How has Catholicism changed and adapted to such vast and diverse cultural influences over the centuries? What great challenges does the Catholic Church now face in the twenty-first century, both within its own life and in its relation to others around the world? In this Very Short Introduction, Gerald O'Collins draws on the best current scholarship available to answer these questions and to present, in clear and accessible language, a fresh introduction to the largest and oldest institution in the world.

www.oup.com/vsi

PAGANISM
A Very Short Introduction
Owen Davies

This *Very Short Introduction* explores the meaning of paganism - through a chronological overview of the attitudes towards its practices and beliefs - from the ancient world through to the present day. Owen Davies largely looks at paganism through the eyes of the Christian world, and how, over the centuries, notions and representations of its nature were shaped by religious conflict, power struggles, colonialism, and scholarship. Despite the expansion of Christianity and Islam, Pagan cultures continue to exist around the world, whilst in the West new formations of paganism constitute one of the fastest-growing religions.

CLASSICAL MYTHOLOGY
A Very Short Introduction
Helen Morales

From Zeus and Europa, to Diana, Pan, and Prometheus, the myths of ancient Greece and Rome seem to exert a timeless power over us. But what do those myths represent, and why are they so enduringly fascinating? This imaginative and stimulating *Very Short Introduction* is a wide-ranging account, examining how classical myths are used and understood in both high art and popular culture, taking the reader from the temples of Crete to skyscrapers in New York, and finding classical myths in a variety of unexpected places: from Arabic poetry and Hollywood films, to psychoanalysis, the bible, and New Age spiritualism.

www.oup.com/vsi

FREE SPEECH
A Very Short Introduction
Nigel Warburton

'I disapprove of what you say, but I will defend to the death your right to say it' This slogan, attributed to Voltaire, is frequently quoted by defenders of free speech. Yet it is rare to find anyone prepared to defend all expression in every circumstance, especially if the views expressed incite violence. So where do the limits lie? What is the real value of free speech? Here, Nigel Warburton offers a concise guide to important questions facing modern society about the value and limits of free speech: Where should a civilized society draw the line? Should we be free to offend other people's religion? Are there good grounds for censoring pornography? Has the Internet changed everything? This Very Short Introduction is a thought-provoking, accessible, and up-to-date examination of the liberal assumption that free speech is worth preserving at any cost.

> 'The genius of Nigel Warburton's *Free Speech* lies not only in its extraordinary clarity and incisiveness. Just as important is the way Warburton addresses freedom of speech - and attempts to stifle it - as an issue for the 21st century. More than ever, we need this book.'
>
> Denis Dutton, University of Canterbury, New Zealand